P.D.JAMES

RECOGNITIONS

Bruce Cassiday, General Editor

detective/suspense

Dorothy L. Sayers
By Dawson Gaillard

Raymond Chandler
By Jerry Speir

Ross Macdonald
By Jerry Speir

Sons of Sam Spade: The Private Eye Novel in the 1970s
By David Geherin

Also of interest

The Bedside, Bathtub & Armchair Companion to Agatha Christie
Edited by Dick Riley and Pam McAllister
Introduction by Julian Symons

science fiction

Critical Encounters: Writers and Themes in Science Fiction
Edited by Dick Riley

Frank Herbert
By Timothy O'Reilly

Ray Bradbury
By Wayne L. Johnson

Theodore Sturgeon
By Lucy Menger

Ursula K. Le Guin
By Barbara F. Bucknall

P.D.JAMES

NORMA SIEBENHELLER

FREDERICK UNGAR PUBLISHING CO.
NEW YORK

Copyright © 1981 by Frederick Ungar Publishing Co.
Printed in the United States of America

Library of Congress Cataloging in Publication Data

Siebenheller, Norma.
P. D. James.

(Recognitions series)
Bibliography: p.
Includes index.
  1. James, P. D.—Criticism and interpretation.
I. Title. II. Series.
PR6060.A467Z88   823'.914   81-40473
ISBN 0-8044-2817-4   AACR2
ISBN 0-8044-6862-1 (pbk.)

TO BILL

who has made everything possible

CONTENTS

PREFACE

P.D. James is a novelist who happens to write in the mystery form. That distinction—endorsed by the writer herself—is not merely semantic; it is, in fact, what this book is all about.

Her plots, while appropriate to novels that deal with crime, transcend the mere puzzle aspect of the traditional mystery. Her characters have a depth that is neither necessary to nor common in the genre, and her themes strike chords of recognition in a wide audience. Who has not grappled with loneliness, been affronted by the terrible certainty of death, harbored thoughts—however brief—of retribution? Who has not wondered about his true identity? Who has never been touched by crime?

These are matters that concern most thinking people. P.D. James deals with them in such a way as to please both the conventional mystery buff and an ever-increasing general readership as well. She entertains, yes, but she also gives us a lot to think about, even after she's told us "whodunit."

Her body of work is small enough—eight novels over a period of twenty years—to allow me to treat it in its entirety rather than to select only the highlights for discussion. Thus I have given rather detailed plot summaries in the early chapters, taking the books in chronological order, before focusing on the specifics of characterization, major themes, and literary style.

A word of warning: I have found it necessary in almost all cases to reveal the identities of the culprits. It would have been impossible to present an intelligent analysis of the work without doing so. The reader who wishes to maintain the element of surprise is urged to read all of James's books before embarking on this one.

I worked primarily from paperback copies of the novels since these were the more readily available. In 1980 only *Innocent Blood* and *The Black Tower* were still in print in original hardcover editions, although three other titles (*Cover Her Face, A Mind to Murder*, and *Shroud for a Nightingale*) could be found in a 1979 compendium entitled *Crime Times Three*, and several of the stories have begun to appear in large-print editions. The page numbers given in the notes at the end of this volume reflect the paperback editions, except for the last, *Innocent Blood*.

Careful scrutiny of the P.D. James entry in *Who's Who* will reveal one title credited to her that has not been dealt with in these pages. It is *The Maul and the Pear Tree*, written jointly by P.D. James and Thomas A. Critchley, and it is her only nonfiction effort. It concerns a series of real crimes, the "Radcliffe Highway Murders", that took place in 1811 in London's East End. Because it was not fiction—and also because it has not been published in the United States—*The Maul and the Pear Tree* has been omitted from my discussion.

In researching this book, I found that very little had been written to date about P.D. James. A few short articles in newspapers or magazines, some basic biographical facts in *Who's Who*, a number of reviews—that was all. For this reason I am especially grateful to Mrs. James for taking the time to telephone me while she was in New York in June 1980 and for clarifying her positions for me on many issues during that talk. Her generous gift of time was a very real help to me in the preparation of this work.

I want also to thank Dick Riley, who has guided this book so expertly from beginning to end. Without his patient encouragement I would not be writing these words today.

N.S.

New York
February 1981

1

OVERVIEW

Phyllis Dorothy James was born on August 3, 1920, in Oxford, England, the daughter of Sidney and Dorothy James. Her upbringing was English middle-class. She graduated from secondary school in Cambridge but did not go on to a university since, as she has remarked, higher education was not subsidized and, "My father was not disposed to educate girls." Her first job, at the age of sixteen, was in a local tax office, a position she left after a few years to work as an assistant stage manager at the Festival Theater in Cambridge.

At twenty-one she was married to a physician, Ernest Connor White, with whom she had two daughters, born in 1942 and 1944. Dr. White served in England's armed forces during World War II and returned home in 1945 seriously ill with schizophrenia. He was never really well again and died in 1964. Out of financial necessity his wife went to work in 1949 for the newly formed National Health Service, and during her years of service there she rose through the ranks to the position of hospital administrator. The extensive grounding she thus received in all aspects of illness,

1

medicine, hospital procedure, and laboratory technique has enabled her to use medically related institutions as backgrounds to her stories with convincing detail and believability. Her understanding of the medical world, so intriguing and so baffling to much of the public, and her compassion for the sick and for those who must cope with the sick, have become hallmarks of her work.

In 1968 Phyllis James White left hospital administration "to broaden my horizons," selecting the Criminal Division of the British Home Office as her field of interest after passing a highly competitive examination for senior-level placement.

She became a specialist in juvenile delinquency. The insight she gained from this job—which she continued until the end of 1979—gave her work a new dimension. She became as well versed in criminal procedure and criminal behavior as she was in all the many facets of medicine and illness.

All of her books have made use, to some extent, of these areas of expertise, and this is one of the reasons she has been credited with creating such "real" settings for her stories. One certainly gets the feeling that the writer is an insider—which she is.

Unlike many writers, P.D. James came to the profession rather late in life. She was thirty-nine when she began her first novel, *Cover Her Face*, and by her own admission had written little prior to that time. The urge to do so, however, had been present since childhood.

"I feared that, if I didn't settle down and write a novel, I'd end up an old lady telling my children and grandchildren that I had always wanted to be a writer," she remarked many years later. And so, despite the demands of a full-time job, a family, and a sick husband, she began.

The book took three years to complete, but it was accepted immediately for publication under the nom de plume "P.D. James." The use of her maiden name, while her husband was still alive, indicates James's strong feelings of personal identity. At her job she was Mrs. White, but in her books, which would contain her own creations and her own philosophies, she would use her own name. "It is the essential me," she has said.

Her use of initials instead of her first name was deliberately designed to be sexually ambiguous. She never made any attempt to hide her true identity, but she did use this means to avoid becoming labeled as a "woman writer" at the very outset of her career.

James never had to struggle with the demons of rejection and revision that are the lot of many writers of novels, even ultimately successful ones. *Cover Her Face* was accepted by the first house to whom it was offered, Faber and Faber in London, and the same firm is still her British publisher. Scribner's is her publisher in the United States.

Her success was modest at first, but over the years she built a regular following among mystery fans who quickly became attached to her intellectual, sensitive detective, Adam Dalgleish. Dalgleish is a professional, with the Detective Division of Scotland Yard, and he is a far cry from the almost comical characters who served Christie and Sayers as sleuths. He is neither amusing nor omnipotent; he is just a detective, albeit a superior one, doing his job. He takes that job very seriously and lets nothing interfere with the proper execution of it.

James was determined from the beginning to create a "real" detective to solve her fictional crimes. She feels very strongly that death is a serious matter and should be written about seriously, even within the confines of the mystery novel.

Thus it was inevitable that her principal character be a man and a professional policeman. Most murders are solved by police and not by "private eyes," and they are generally solved with standard police procedures rather than by sudden, quirky insights or revelations. And, too, most police—then and now—are men. So, for optimum believability, her sleuth had to be a policeman, and given the British system it is only natural that she placed him at Scotland Yard.

Unlike some paper detectives Adam Dalgleish has aged with each book, reflecting at least in part the actual passage of years. He has developed (and broken) relationships with other recurring characters. And he has risen in rank as one would naturally expect him to do, from Detective-Commander to Detective Chief-Inspector. Yet he has not greatly changed for all that; he is today essentially the same man he was in *Cover Her Face*: introspective, compulsive, devoted to his work, sensitive to the feelings of others, yet withdrawn into himself. All these characteristics were made known in the first novel, and they are not substantially different today.

Many crime novels are written in the first person, with the detective as narrator, or in the first person plural, with the sleuth's confidant—his "Watson"—detailing the activities step by step. James does not take this tack; instead she uses the third person, shifting points of view to give the reader a wider view of the scene. This technique is more difficult to do well than the first person method, and James's mastery of it is one reason she is considered by many critics a complete novelist rather than simply a crime writer.

The comparisons between her and Agatha Christie, which have become frequent since Christie's death, are overdrawn and misdirected. But, of course, she is English; she is a woman; she does write mysteries. Where does she stand in the ranks of the others who share these three traits?

The classic English mystery, as practiced by many of its female creators, is basically a puzzle-solving exercise. It is a steeplechase of clues, false and true. There is murder, to be sure, but it rarely involves people's emotions or causes real pain. Characters, except for a few, are two-dimensional. Setting, atmosphere, and mood are all subordinate to the main event, which is the plot. The more devious and convoluted the story, the more successful is the book. Whether an ending is believable or not is not really important; what matters are the twists and turns along the way. It is, most of all, fun.

Agatha Christie popularized the style and Dorothy Sayers, Josephine Tey, Ngaio Marsh and Margery Allingham, among others, have carried it on and stretched it in several directions. Each has her own recurring character or characters who are developed over a period of years. Some, like Christie's Miss Marple or Hercule Poirot, are comically unreal. Others, like Sayers's Peter Wimsey, are more rounded and yet still totally fictional. Only Tey's Inspector Grant and Marsh's Roderick Alleyn seem like real people put on paper—perhaps because they (like Dalgleish) are professional policemen, solving crimes as part of their job and not, like Wimsey or Marple, simply because they keep happening upon them. And they solve them, in most cases, with legwork and police methodology, not by using their "little gray cells" or vague parallels to the past.

Marsh and Allingham, especially, fleshed out their stories with description to a far greater degree than did Christie, and Sayers's classical training was often reflected in her stories. Yet their books are still basically puzzles. One never gets over the feeling, when reading these books, that they are all make-believe—that, when the action is over and the murderer named, the victim will get up, brush himself off, and carry on with his life.

P.D. James departs from that tradition. Her concern is with reality, not make-believe. The worlds she creates are peopled with varied and interesting characters whose actions spring from believable motivations and whose reactions are true to their complex personalities. And her victims, as she has often remarked, are truly dead.

Yet, if P.D. James does not strictly walk in the footsteps of the earlier English women of mystery, she does, in her mystery stories, uphold some of their traditions. Her work is literate, tightly constructed, and civilized. Her people are genteel and polite. Her favorite author is Jane Austen, and the order and sanity present in Austen's work is reflected in James's. She is not at home with violence or physical conflict; the few times she has tried to incorporate these things into her stories, she has fallen into melodramatic excess. Her strength is in her civility. The lack of rough-and-tumble action in her books is more than balanced by her inventive characterizations, her psychological insights, and her superbly detailed descriptions.

While James is both different from and similar to the other female writers of the English school, she is totally unlike the American practitioners of the mystery genre. With most of the English writers, plot is all-important, but in the American private-eye story the true subject is the hard-boiled, free-swinging detective himself. The books are usually first-person narratives and are filled with tough talk and rough action. Sex, which is discreetly absent from most English mysteries, is liberally included in American ones. The civility and order that pervade the English stories— including James's—are missing. Mystery readers generally like one or the other style, seldom both. Those who devour Hammett, Chandler, and Macdonald may find P.D. James's work rather tame.

She stresses neither her plot (twisted though it may be) nor her detective (interesting as he is). In James's work, crime itself is the focus, not just the murder, but its effects on all who are touched by it. This corrosive, destructive aspect of crime, the way it shatters the lives not only of the criminal and the victim but also of their families, their friends, and other innocent people ensnared in its net, is a major James theme, and one she returns to in each of her books.

It sets her apart, not only from those women writers with whom she is most often compared, but from other mystery writers as well. It has brought her, in fact, beyond the mystery novel, into the realm of general popular fiction.

2

THREE NOVELS OF THE SIXTIES
Cover Her Face
A Mind to Murder
Unnatural Causes

Although P.D. James had never written for publication before commencing work on her first novel, she displayed from the beginning a thorough professionalism, a command of her craft that is usually the result of years of apprenticeship. That is not to say, however, that she has not grown since. She certainly has; the work of the 1970s and 1980s is more mature than that of her earlier years, more subtle, more complex. In that sense, the 1960s may be viewed as her learning years.

In that decade she produced three books: *Cover Her Face, A Mind to Murder,* and *Unnatural Causes.* Individually and as a group they mark the first steps on James's journey toward recognition as a serious novelist, as well as an excellent mystery writer.

COVER HER FACE

The average reader, unfamiliar with James and coming upon this book without prior expectations, may think at the beginning that it is not a mystery at all but a modern Gothic. It certainly has a

Gothic flavor at the start: a grand old English house in the countryside, its patriarch slowly dying upstairs; Stephen Maxie, the son and heir, an outwardly cold and distant young man, though physically attractive; Sally Jupp, a young and pretty girl in reduced circumstances who is working for the family as a maid. In addition there is Catherine Bowers, a capable but uninteresting young woman in love with Stephen; Deborah Riscoe, Stephen's very possessive twin sister; and Felix Hearne, Deborah's would-be fiance. Together they comprise all the ingredients of a classic Gothic confrontation.

It does not, however, occur, for after this basic introduction the tone changes abruptly when Sally—who would have to have been the heroine, in any happily-ever-after romance—is strangled in her bed on the very night she has triumphantly declared to the family her intention of marrying Stephen. Her death effectively diverts this book from its formula track and onto a separate road, the road of the mystery. From that point on the object of the story is not romance, but problem-solving. It is a measure of James's innate, unpracticed abilities that she brings off the ending quite well indeed. at least as far as the surprise element of it is concerned.

The death of Sally Jupp is not the tragic event it would have been had the story been conceived as a Gothic romance. Like other James victims in the early books, Sally is a very unsympathetic character.

She has, it is made clear at the book's beginning, "made a mistake"—a euphemistic way of saying in the 1950s (when the book was actually begun) that she was unlucky enough to find herself with child and without a husband. She refused to name the man responsible and did the only sensible thing open to a girl in her situation at that time: she entered a charitable home for unwed mothers, St. Mary's Refuge for Girls. There she was cared for until the child was born; from there she was "guided" into the job as assistant housemaid in the Maxie household. All concerned—Miss Liddell, warden of St. Mary's; Mrs. Maxie Senior, mistress of Martingale, the Maxie estate; and the local Vicar, who felt himself morally responsible—were very proud of their openmindedness in "rescuing" Sally from her wayward path and setting her straight again.

Sally herself had no choice but to accept this moralistic inter-ference in her life, but she secretly held them all in contempt. She was never the contrite, repentant little thing they all wanted her to be. In Catherine Bowers's words, "I always thought she was sly. She never seemed the least grateful for all that the family had done for her." She wasn't. She was too busy scheming about how she would get back at them all.

If the fact of Sally's "sin" is supposed to help define her unpleasant character, it fails utterly in an easier moral climate, when changing sexual mores have removed any stigma once associated with out-of-wedlock conception. Nevertheless there are enough later illustrations of Sally's selfish, manipulative character to paint her in harsh colors; the fact of her unwed motherhood becomes simply an element in the plot. The righteous tone of the early pages, so dated now, is soon superseded by the murder and the painstaking solving of it.

To aid in that solving, James introduces Adam Dalgleish of Scotland Yard, the complex, intriguing detective who is subse-quently featured in the next six of her books. Even in this first appearance Dalgleish is quite fully developed; he had obviously been solidly constructed in James's mind before he ever appeared on the printed page. His rank, in this first venture, is Detective Chief-Inspector. He isn't directly described, in a physical sense, but is seen through the eyes of others in the household:

> Catherine Bowers thought, "Tall, dark and handsome. Not what I expected. Quite an interesting face really." Stephen Maxie thought, "Supercilious-looking devil . . ." Felix Hearne thought, "Adam Dal-gleish, I've heard of him. Ruthless, unorthodox, working always against time. . . . At least they've thought us adversaries worthy of the best." Eleanor Maxie thought, "Where have I seen that head before? Of course. That Durer. Portrait of an Unknown Man. Why does one always expect police officers to wear raincoats . . ."

So gradually Dalgleish emerges. He is merciless in his pursuit of truth, yet compassionate toward those into whose lives he must intrude. He is totally in control, both of himself and of a given situation, confident of success, yet seized always by the self-doubts of an introspective personality. He is single, unattached—detached, actually—sensitive, artistic; in short, he is an interesting man, though not entirely a likeable one.

Since the murder has taken place at night, when a given number of known individuals were staying at Martingale, the list of suspects is initially small. However, the estate's grounds had been open to the public on the previous day for the annual church fete, which brought a number of outsiders to the scene, at least one of whom was seen trying to enter the house. And the fact that a ladder had been placed against Sally's second-story window lends credence to the theory that the killer had not come from the house. Inquiries are made: to the publishing house in London where Sally had once worked, to the young local boy she met with surreptitiously, to the aunt and uncle who had—somewhat grudgingly—raised her after her parents were killed in the war. Little by little the threads unravel, until a much larger group than was originally indicated is caught up in suspicion.

The Sally that emerges, from all her acquaintances' descriptions, was a manipulative person, and one of those she manipulated was Miss Liddell, who later said to Dalgleish, "She must have been laughing at me all the time. I suppose you think I'm a fool . . ." Miss Malpas of the Select Book Club, where Sally had once worked before her pregnancy, was more objective:

> "Sally Jupp was pretty, intelligent, ambitious, sly, and insecure," she said. "She wasn't easy to know. . . . She had [the rest of the staff] eating out of her hand, of course. They bought her birthday and Christmas presents. She even asked for advice about her clothes! As if she cared a damn what we wore or what we thought! . . . After a few months of Sally we'd got an office atmosphere . . . tensions, barbed remarks, unexplained feuds. . . . She'd got them all in a tizzy of jealousy, and the poor fools couldn't see it."

And Sally had stood apart, like a stage director, planning the next move. ·

Her uncle had nothing good to say about her either. She had been extorting money from him, threatening to sue for a small inheritance he had mismanaged.

> "I was on a string all right," he told Dalgleish. "But I knew what she was up to. If she'd tried it again I'd go to the police."
>
> "She wouldn't have." Deborah broke in. "She was only playing with you. . . . The real attraction was seeing you sweat . . ."

Yet Sally had her good points. Little Jimmy, her son, was well cared for; there was no doubt she was a loving mother. Dalgleish feels that the key to her murder lies, somehow, with the father of her child; if he can be identified, then other seemingly inexplicable pieces of the puzzle might fall into place. Sally's sometimes bizarre behavior cannot be fully understood until the identity of Jimmy's father is known.

James scatters clues quite liberally throughout the course of the story and manages to dangle a few red herrings to distract the reader, all in the best tradition of the classic mystery. A particularly clever device is the apparent relationship between clues that in fact have no relation to each other. Sally's cocoa, it is discovered, was drugged on the night of her murder, and that fact made it easier for the murderer to subdue her. Attention naturally centers on why a certain drug was used, on who had access to it, and finally on who could have slipped it into the drink—but it is up to Dalgleish to discover that the drugging and the strangling are unrelated, done by different persons for different reasons, and not until this fact is made clear can the search for the murderer begin in earnest.

Not quite so neatly done is the actual denouement. The clues have been clearly laid, and the solution is logical, but it is not necessarily believable. One can't help wondering if Mrs. Maxie could really have reacted violently, no matter how threatened she felt by Sally. Perhaps so; strong emotions are very powerful spurs to action, and murders have been committed by far less likely people. Yet there is something unsatisfying about this story's end.

Cover Her Face (the title derives from Webster's *Duchess of Malfi*: "Cover her face: Mine eyes dazzle; she died young.") is in many ways a very dated book, yet it is no less interesting despite that. The mystery reader does not require Shakespearean timelessness in his selections, and it is the plot, not the external trappings, that make a book readable or not. On that basis *Cover Her Face* does succeed, its 1950s morality, which seems so curiously far away, notwithstanding.

But still—and especially considering what James has achieved since—*Cover Her Face* can be seen as a first effort, a trying-out of style, substance, method. The tied-up ending, for example, where James spins the story out far beyond its natural finish, in order to explain what happened to the rest of the characters, is old-fashioned and, in the end, unnecessary.

One mustn't, when discussing *Cover Her Face*, neglect to mention one other important thing, and that is the role of Deborah Riscoe. Stephen Maxie's twin sister, Deborah is a young widow who is stunningly attractive, intelligent, self-interested, and very much drawn to the enigmatic Adam Dalgleish. Even her early dislike of him is tempered by her knowledge that she would like to know him better, and at the book's finish it becomes obvious that Dalgleish feels the same way. He is a widower—his wife died in childbirth early in their marriage, their child with her—and in the years since he has been afraid of caring for anyone. But he suspects that he may one day care for Deborah. The very last lines in the book—". . . he knew with sudden and heart-lifting certainty that they would meet again. And when that happened the right words would be found"—indicate that James had already decided that Dalgleish would be her major recurring character and sus-pected that Deborah would somehow be involved with him on a continuing basis. The breadth and depth of that relationship is left to a future novel to explore.

A MIND TO MURDER

In *Cover Her Face* James may in some ways have dealt with a stock situation—albeit with a twist—but in *A Mind to Murder* she comes into her own as an innovative writer, creating and describing a world very different from the standard English country house.

For the first time in what has become a major trend on her part, James uses a hospital (in this case, a clinic) setting for her story. The central characters are the doctors, nurses, administrators, orderlies, and patients who people this world; they are a rich and varied lot, as in real life any such group would be. They come from vastly differing backgrounds, have motives, drives, and fears that are far deeper than those ordinarily encountered in mysteries, and leave impressions that stay with the reader long after the basic twists of plot have been forgotten.

This is, in short, a book about people—people who just happen to get caught up in a murder.

The setting is the fashionable Steen Clinic in London, a privately endowed psychiatric outpatient facility, which has managed to maintain its independence within the framework of Britain's National Health Service. On a Friday evening, when the clinic is open for carefully monitored LSD treatments of some severe neurotics, and with much of the staff on duty, Enid Bolam, the Steen's administrative officer is murdered—stabbed through the heart with a chisel. Upon the discovery of her body Dr. Etheridge, the medical director, gathers all those present together, orders all exits locked, and calls the police.

Adam Dalgleish, now bearing the rank of Superintendent and attending a party at his publisher's, celebrating the third reprint of his first book of poetry, is summoned from the festivities to direct the investigation. He is there in minutes, and the real business of the book begins.

Three years have passed since Dalgleish's fictional debut. He has risen in his profession; he has remained single (he still mourns his wife, and has just lit a ritual candle on the thirteenth anniversary of her death); and he feels himself—he *fears* himself—on the brink of falling in love with Deborah Riscoe. She, too, was at the publishing party (she works there), and he was just about to say the words that might have spelled the end of his privacy when the Yard called and the murder investigation took precedence. It was not the first time this had happened, nor, one suspects, would it be the last.

Information comes to light bit by bit, as Dalgleish proceeds to interview the principals. The doctors, of whom there are several, are brusque and businesslike, quick to offer alibis for the half-hour time period in question. The rest of the contingent was, unfortunately for each of them, busy at solitary tasks. Any one of them could be a suspect.

Dr. Etheridge immediately offers a ray of light, diffused though it is at first. Miss Bolam had, he says, called him earlier that day to request an interview at his earliest convenience.

"Something was going on at the clinic and she needed advice. I came as soon as I could and found she'd been murdered. . . . It looks as if she needed advice more than she knew."

Dalgleish asks to see the body. The handle of the chisel

. . . had been driven up to the hilt. There was very little bruising of the tissues and no blood. The woman's vest had been rolled up above her breasts to expose the flesh for that vicious, calculated thrust. Such deliberation suggested that the killer had a confident knowledge of anatomy.

Of course, in a psychiatric clinic there are necessarily a lot of people who have a confident knowledge of anatomy. James has quite deftly ensnared all the main characters in her net.

There is the matter of motive: who would benefit by this death? A number of people would, for different reasons, some more obvious than others. There is the dead woman's cousin, Nurse Marion Bolam, who works in the LSD Unit; the two had shared the same grandmother, but the old lady left all her money to Enid and ignored Marion. That money would come to Marion on her cousin's death—at least it would according to the will currently in effect. But Enid Bolam was only forty, and her cousin needed money *now*. Dalgleish wonders whether she would kill to get it. He decides she might.

But, while money may have been the most obvious motive for murder, it was by no means the only one. Many people had reason to dislike or distrust Enid Bolam. As the administrative officer of the Steen she had been capable, efficient, highly conscientious. Group Secretary Reginald Lauder said of her:

"She was competent. . . . I don't think she ever sent in an inaccurate return."

"Poor devil," thought Dalgleish, stung by the bleak anonymity of that official epitaph . . .

She was also fair, in a rule-book sort of way, but she had been stern, unbending, rigid, and cold. She had no thought for feelings and dealt with the affairs of the clinic on a totally impersonal basis. She had no hesitation, for example, in telling the wife of one of the staff doctors that her husband was having an affair with a fellow employee, thus shattering three lives with one quick word.

"She told Mrs. Baguley? That seems an unusually officious and cruel thing to have done."

"It wasn't, really. Bolam wouldn't see it that way. She was one of those rare and fortunate people who never for one moment doubt that they know the difference between right and wrong. . . . If she were a wife whose husband was unfaithful I'm sure that she would want to be told about it. . . . I expect she thought it was her duty to tell."

Dalgleish wonders if any of those three people could have hated Enid Bolam enough to kill her. Other subordinates might have wanted her out of the way because of personality conflicts—doctors don't like administrative officers to make decisions that affect their practice of medicine or, in at least one case, because of a desire to take over her job. The initial interrogation of suspects provides no real clues. There had been a robbery the previous week, but it was an isolated event, puzzling—someone had broken in and taken an envelope containing £15, money that had arrived unexpectedly and inexplicably in the mail only the day before—but isolated. Nothing else had been reported missing, before or since. The medical records might hold a clue. Bolam had been killed in the records room, and files had been strewn about haphazardly. There might be something in that. As for blackmail, Dalgleish can't imagine what its purpose might be, or who might be its victim. Unless it had nothing to do with the clinic at all, but was something personal, something to do with Miss Bolam alone.

Assisted by Sergeant Martin (the same Martin who was Dalgleish's sidekick in *Cover Her Face*) the Superintendent seeks some answers in the dead woman's personal life. She lived alone; they have to search her flat for clues. It is not a task Dalgleish relishes:

> This prying among the personal residue of a finished life was a part of his job which Dalgleish had always found distasteful. It was too much like putting the dead at a disadvantage. During his career he had examined with interest and with pity so many petty leavings. The soiled underclothes pushed hurriedly into drawers . . .

But there is no such embarrassment awaiting him in Enid Bolam's flat. It is obsessively neat and tidy, the clothing clean and carefully hung or folded, photographs labeled, letters filed. She "might have lived each day as if expecting sudden death." It is all very straightforward, very clear; there seem to be no hidden layers to Enid Bolam. She was what she had seemed to be.

She had, Dalgleish discovers from a letter on her desk, been planning to change her will. That puts a stronger weight on the motives of her cousin Marion; perhaps there was a sudden pressure there, after all. But it sheds no light on the mysterious "goings on" that she had wanted to recount to the medical director. And it is in that direction, Dalgleish feels, that his investigations must proceed.

James allows the reader to get to know Dalgleish quite well, but at the crucial moment—when he gets his sudden flashes of insight—the workings of his mind are not revealed. This is the one slight deception in James's generally honest unfolding of plot. It is, however, necessary to the continuing suspense of the story that Dalgleish's thoughts not be revealed too soon. The hunch becomes a device to permit Dalgleish to channel his investigations along certain lines without alerting the reader to his reasons for doing so.

In this case he has a hunch that deals with the matter that must have been on Bolam's mind just before her death. He suddenly realizes what must have been taking place, and why.

Mental illness is different from other illness, in that there is, in the public eye, some stigma attached to it. Many patients never get over the feeling that the whole thing is, somehow, their own fault, and even after a cure is effected a trace of guilt remains. It must be hushed up. Neighbors must be lied to, employers deceived. Some may scoff at these feelings, but they are, nevertheless, quite real for at least some proportion of the ranks of the mentally ill. And if this is so today, it was even more so in the mid-1960s.

Therefore, Dalgleish decides, someone now working at the clinic has found out how to isolate certain cases, in the long-dormant files of the cured, that would be particularly vulnerable to blackmail for the sake of silence: people who had suffered from the most "socially unacceptable" diseases, such as sexual aberrations or kleptomania; who worked at businesses where deviation from the norm was frowned upon; who lived, not in the great tolerant city of London, but in a small gossipy suburb; who would be able to afford a small monthly payment, but not rich enough—nor powerful enough—to stand up to the blackmailer and refuse, or worse, go to the police.

To get any further with his hypothesis, Dalgleish must determine how the various files are coded on the clinic's punch-card index. Someone must be trusted; someone in a position of authority must be taken into his confidence, for Dalgleish knows he can't proceed without help. He decides that, if one person can be ruled out of suspicion immediately, that person is Dr. Etheridge. Dalgleish tells him what he wants:

> "It occurs to me [Doctor] that we have here a neatly contrived apparatus for the preselection of a victim. You push through the rod and out pops a card."
> "What do you want me to do?"
> "To help me select a victim. . . . Now if I were the blackmailer would I choose a man or a woman? If it's a question of a regular income a man is probably a better bet. Let's take the males out next . . ."

And so the selection process goes on, until Dalgleish has a list of ten names of likely "victims." At that point a series of telephone calls, inquiring merely if the former patient had tried to contact the Steen during the past week, turns up, on the fifth try, success:

> "That was the wife of a Colonel Fenton of Sprigg's Green in Kent. She telephoned Miss Bolam about a very serious matter at about midday last Friday. She didn't want to talk to you on the phone about it and I thought it better not to press her. But she'd like to see you as soon as possible. I've written down the address."
> "Thank you, Doctor," said Dalgleish, and took the proferred paper. He showed neither surprise nor relief, but his heart was singing.

It is as he suspected: a telephone call, several years ago, had demanded a small monthly payment for silence, only fifteen pounds, to be sent by the first of each month to the administrative secretary, in an envelope addressed in green ink. The demand never increased, but the one time the payment was late there had been another phone call, rather menacing in nature. Colonel Fenton had been afraid to stop. But now he was ill and had confessed the whole thing to his wife. She called Enid Bolam and demanded the matter be investigated, at once.

Dalgleish is exuberant. He knows the case is not solved yet—knowing is not proving—but he says to Martin: "We've got the motive. This is one of those rare cases in which knowing why is knowing who."

The alert reader at this point will know who, too—until both the reader and Detective Superintendent Dalgleish are proved wrong, in a stunning turn of events at the very end of the story.

James makes good use of the device she used in *Cover Her Face*, that is, of clues that appear to be related, but which in truth are not. The whole episode of the blackmail is an elaborate red herring, and Dalgleish is as much deceived as the reader:

> "It was a perfectly straightforward case" said the A.C. "The obvious suspect, the obvious motive."
> "Too obvious for me, apparently," said Dalgleish bitterly. "If this case doesn't cure me of conceit, nothing will."

It isn't every writer who can get away with creating a major case based on her detective's biggest failure, but James does it handily. The book succeeds on many levels.

The author evokes a strong sense of place; the atmosphere of the clinic is so knowledgeably described that the whole picture emerges as reality. James knows her way around hospitals and clinics from first-hand experience, and she has an understanding of mental illness, from having lived with a schizophrenic husband for many years. This is a book by an insider, and it is stronger because of that fact.

The plotting is clever, the action steady, and the final twist almost certainly a shocker for even the most analytical reader. It is, from that aspect, the most clever of her books; she has never achieved such total surprise since.

The characters are fully realized, the major ones, at any rate— from the avaricious and ambitious Mrs. Bostock, who stood to inherit Bolam's job, to the porter Peter Nagle, a painter of no small merit who would do anything to advance himself in his field, to pretty, vapid Jennifer Priddy, in love with Nagle and ready to sacrifice anything—or anyone—who might threaten him, and Enid Bolam herself, obsessive, pathetic Enid Bolam.

Dalgleish, too, is further defined in this book. Not the least important characteristic that emerges is the man's fallibility; the remembrance of it, and the self-doubts that it produces, will color his actions in the future. He frequently wishes he could be one of those confident individuals who never question the wisdom of their actions. That he isn't is just one more measure of his believability.

The book begins with his being "saved," by murder, from involvement with Deborah Riscoe, an involvement he both wants and fears. When the story ends, she is back in the picture. Dalgleish is filled with a sour self-pity because of his failure in the Bolam murder.

> If he were to break free from this pervasive gloom he needed a respite from crime and death, needed to walk for one brief evening out of the shadow of blackmail and murder. It came to him that what he wanted was to dine with Deborah Riscoe. At least, he told himself wryly, it would be a change of trouble.

It is, as well, a bridge to the third novel: *Unnatural Causes*.

UNNATURAL CAUSES

A year has passed. Dalgleish acted on that impulse to call Deborah, and has pursued the relationship to the apparent satisfaction of both. Things have now progressed to a point where a decision of some kind must be made. Shall it be permanent? Or shall it end? The choice is not an easy one for Dalgleish, with years of studied detachment behind him, to make. He has put it off as long as possible but it can be postponed no longer. He is embarking on a ten-day holiday in Suffolk with his only living relative, his spinster Aunt Jane, and he knows that, before he returns to London, he must choose: marriage or privacy, Deborah—or Adam.

But there is little time to brood over personal entanglements. Dalgleish has no sooner arrived than the little coastal settlement of Monksmere is plunged into, first, a disappearance, and then a murder. And, while it is truly a matter for the local police and not a vacationing Detective-Superintendent, he finds it difficult to stay out of the ensuing investigations. Aunt Jane may even, by a long stretch of provincial imagination, be considered a suspect, and he has to seek out the truth, if only to clear her from any association with the crime.

The fact of a murder is established on the very first page of the book, in the first sentence in fact, as James tries a "grabber" of a lead for the first time: "The corpse without hands lay in the bottom of a small sailing dinghy drifting just within sight of the Suffolk coast. It was the body of a middle-aged man . . ." After this plunge into mayhem in its very first line, the story moves on to reveal who the victim is, who killed him, and, finally, why his hands are missing.

As in the first two novels, the author uses the device of a closed community. As the first book centered on Martingale, and the second on the Steen Clinic, so this third one focuses on the community at Monksmere Head. It contains an odd assortment of people. It is essentially a literary retreat, this quiet, secluded spot on the cliffs overlooking the North Sea. Jane Dalgleish is not a writer—she chose her home, Pentlands, for its proximity to the Bird Sanctuary—but most of her neighbors are. Jane's famous nephew, who has just published his second book of poetry, fits right in.

Among the Monksmere residents are Celia Calthrop, who lives at Rosemary Cottage and writes popular romances, and R.B. Sinclair, at Priory House, still basking in the glow of three excellent novels written some thirty years before. Oliver Latham, a dramatic critic, lives in a little stone cottage on the headland, and Justin Bryce, a playwright, is next door. The famous mystery novelist Maurice Seton keeps a weekend cottage nearby. Only Calthrop's niece, Elizabeth Marley, Seton's half-brother Digby Seton, and his crippled secretary Sylvia Kedge are not connected directly to the literary life.

They have all lived or visited at Monksmere Head for a number of years and so know each other somewhat too well, as people in very small towns are apt to do. And under their surface veneer of concern for each other run deeper veins of jealousy, mutual disgust, even hatred, which have lain buried for years. The murder is a volcanic eruption, which allows all these emotions, buried under pressure for so long, to spew forth. The ensuing rain of fire touches nearly everyone, and there are two more deaths before the book is over.

It is Dalgleish's first night at Pentlands, and he and Jane are sitting comfortably by the fire, preparing to listen to her new Mahler recording. Music is one of his aunt's enthusiasms, and, though Dalgleish himself has little feeling for it, he is happy to take part in what has become a ritual between them. This night, to their distress, their quiet is interrupted by the arrival of neighbors, five of them: Celia Calthrop and Elizabeth, Justin Bryce, Oliver Latham, and even Sylvia Kedge, who gets about with great difficulty due to her deformed, heavily braced legs. There is a bit of fuss settling Sylvia, who wears her usual air of "suffering, meekly and uncomplainingly borne," but finally they announce their mission:

> Celia Calthrop had appointed herself spokesman. "It's too bad to come worrying you and Jane on your first evening together. . . . But we're very worried. At least Sylvia and I are. Deeply concerned."
>
> "While I," said Justin Bryce, "am not so much worried as intrigued, not to say hopeful. Maurice Seton's disappeared. I'm afraid it may only be a publicity stunt for his next thriller and that we shall see him among us again all too soon. But let us not look on the gloomy side."

Justin Bryce, thought Dalgleish, is a caricature. But the playwright goes on: "Lost, believed safe. One middle-aged detective writer. Nervous disposition. . . . Finder, please keep. So we come to you for advice, dear boy. Do we . . . ask the police to help us find him?"

They all talk at once. Seton had gone to London on Monday for his annual two-week stay at the Cadaver Club. Sylvia expected to hear from him in the next day or two regarding his current manuscript, but didn't. Then the manager of the club called to say his room hadn't been slept in—and then the manuscript arrived. Sylvia explains: "That isn't his work, Mr. Dalgleish. He didn't write it and he didn't type it."

Dalgleish hardly has time for a response. There is a sharp knock on the door: two local policemen, come to ask a few questions of their own—because Maurice Seton's body has just drifted ashore in a dinghy. With both hands cut off, at the wrists.

That it is foul play there is no doubt, though details are fuzzy at first. Inspector Reckless of the County C.I.D has taken charge, and Dalgleish is placed in the unfamiliar position of being a fifth wheel. Reckless does not defer to him as a less-confident man might have done; in truth, he resents the presence of this famous Scotland Yard sleuth and is not too good at hiding that fact. Dalgleish, for his part, is very uncomfortable in his secondary role. Even when Reckless invites him to be present at a preliminary search of Seton's house, Dalgleish is very nearly rude:

> "He says he is at Seton's house and would be glad if you would join him there this morning."

"He didn't say in what capacity, I suppose? Am I supposed to work, or merely admire him working?"

The great detective does not take easily to the back seat, even on a vacation.

Investigation discloses that Seton, whose wife had killed herself some years previously and who had no children, has left his estate of more than £ 200,000 to his half-brother Digby, in trust, until Digby marries, and absolutely thereafter. Since Digby is something of a ne'er-do-well, generally in need of money to some degree, this might be construed as a motive for murder. And so it is, until it is discovered, after the time of death is established, that Digby was quite clearly and safely in jail, very obviously drunk.

The mystery deepens when it is discovered that Seton died of "natural causes." He had had a heart attack! Why, then, the elaborate scheme involving the dinghy? How and why was the body brought to Monksmere from London? Any why were the hands removed? There seem to be no answers at all to these questions.

The search branches out to London, to a seedy little club in Soho that Seton had visited on the night before his death, to a taxi ride later that evening, and to his destination at Paddington Station. There the trail ends. He died about two hours later.

Reckless seems to think that all the rest—all that elaborate charade with the hands, and the dinghy—is due to a malicious sense of humor on the part of someone, probably someone at Monksmere, who had reason enough to hate Maurice Seton, although not necessarily to kill him. And it seems that nearly all of them did hate him, for real or imagined causes: Celia Calthrop, because he had rebuffed her after his wife's death; Justin Bryce, because he thought Seton had killed his pet cat; Latham, because he felt Seton had driven his wife to suicide; Sylvia Kedge, because she thought he saw her as a sexless machine, cut off by the illness that had crippled and disfigured her legs from any consideration as a full human being. The reasons why Maurice Seton was disliked were almost as many as the number of people who were consulted on the subject. Like James's victims in her first two books, Seton is a very unsympathetic character—not, perhaps, deserving of murder, but not a very nice person in anyone's view.

Dalgleish cannot argue with any of the evidence turned up by Reckless and his men, but he disagrees with their conclusions. He is convinced that they are dealing with a murder, though he cannot conceive of how it was done, and at the first opportunity he goes up to London to do a little sleuthing. He would not interfere with Reckless, but there is nothing to stop his making a few discoveries on his own.

Discover, he does. That, for example, Seton was about to change his will—had already worked out preliminary arrangements, though nothing had been signed—and would soon have disinherited his half-brother in favor of establishing a literary prize. Can Digby have known of this?

He also discovers that Digby's London address, which no one at Monksmere seems to have known, is only a short way from Paddington Station.

And then comes a flash of intuition, one of the sudden hunches for which Dalgleish has become renowned among his colleagues:

> He had been thinking drowsily and without effort of Seton's murder. It had been no more than the mind's slow recapitulation of the past day. And suddenly, inexplicably, he knew how it could have been done.

The reader may well wonder how Dalgleish gets this flash of insight. Is James playing fair, or is Adam Dalgleish relying on superhuman, or at least extrasensory, powers?

True, there are several subtle hints that point toward the murderer, unlikely though that person is, but nowhere does James really disclose just what gave the Superintendent the certain knowledge of the murder method, which is nothing if not ingenious. He may have deduced it from the fact of the severed hands, but then an inventive person could think up half a dozen reasons for that disfigurement, any one of which might have been the correct one. The reader is left to wonder how he *knew*.

There is no answer. He knows—and, knowing, is not totally surprised when the second death occurs. For Digby Seton is dead of poison, in an isolated little hut on the beach.

Has the case against Digby Seton, then, been a red herring? Better, even, than that—the *apparent* red herring is the red herring . . .

Digby *is* one-half of the murder team—the physical half. The planning, the scheming, the organization, all are done by the only other person in Monksmere who had motive, means, and opportunity: Sylvia Kedge.

She knew her employer intimately, from years of close association. She knew his weaknesses and fears and could maneuver the arrival of letters and manuscripts, some of which served as clues (or red herrings) along the way. And she hated him—hated him even more than she hated the rest of humanity, which was a good deal.

What would she gain? More, much more than the satisfaction of carrying out such a "perfect crime." Sylvia would gain wealth—for she has secretly married Seton's heir, Digby Seton, who could not inherit absolutely until he had a wife.

The lure of £200,000 is so strong that Digby allows himself to be drawn into Sylvia's scheme both for the murder, and for the marriage, although he dislikes her as much as does everyone else who knows her. It is not just that, as a cripple, she disgusts him physically, though there is some of that, to be sure. Worse still, she seems to invite dislike, to ask for it. She assumes, in all her human relations, that the other party finds her repellent, and that assumption becomes a self-fulfilling prophecy. People do not really pity Sylvia, though at first they seem to. In truth, they hate her for confronting them with such a *demand* for pity. How dare she command one's compassion? Why does she make everyone feel so uncomfortable, so undeserving of his own good health?

Sylvia is a despicable person. She uses her affliction as a weapon against the world. Her manner is continually saying, "Look at me! Am I not horrible, repellent, disgusting?" In the face of such a barrage, the world comes to agree with her assessment of herself—and she hates them for it. She hates everyone, but she hated Maurice Seton a little bit more than most.

Sylvia, of course, never has any intention of living as Digby Seton's wife. She despises him for a fool and takes advantage of his penchant for drinking whiskey out of a flask to slip him the poison she knows will finish him off. A little arsenic in the flask, a mysterious message designed to draw him deep into the wilds of the Bird Sanctuary (where Adam and Aunt Jane come upon his body some hours later), and Sylvia is suddenly a rich widow. Except at that point no one knows she is married.

It was very nearly the perfect crime, but for the fact that Oliver Latham had seen her and Digby launching the boat on the day after the murder, and guessed the secret. There is a frantic climax scene when, during a violent storm that threatens Sylvia's low-lying house, Adam goes to the rescue and discovers Latham already there. Sylvia claims he tried to attack her, but as the three scramble onto the roof to escape the surging tide, the truth emerges. She tries to force them both into the water, using her crutches and metal braces for the job. She very nearly succeeds, but in the end it is she who is swept away, and the two men are saved. At the last Dalgleish manages to grab the bag she had slung around her neck. In it is confirmation of his theories—and enlightenment for the befuddled reader—in the form of a wedding ring, a marriage certificate, and a taped confession.

A rather dirty trick, on James's part, but then it *was* a perfect crime, and nothing could ever have been proved against her—or against Digby either, for that matter. For Maurice Seton really did die a "natural" death of heart failure. He had been frightened to death.

Sylvia has told all on that tape, which Adam plays for the assembled throng the next day. She alone had known her employer's terrible secret, that he suffered from a recurring dream of being buried alive, a dream from which he would awaken screaming, in claustrophobic terror. It was she who planned with Digby how to execute the crime, a scheme that involved luring Maurice to Digby's flat, knocking him out, and placing him alive in the sidecar of a motorcycle. The actual death would come later, when Seton awoke, and found his nightmare had come true. By that time his half-brother was obviously drunk and safely jailed, and Sylvia, of course, was miles away in Monksmere.

It wasn't until the next day that Digby, in disguise, drove the cycle, with its body, to Monksmere for the dinghy launching, a whimsical touch designed to throw a cloak of confusion over the proceedings. Sylvia thought that the bitterness indicated by that act, and by the cutting off of the hands, might direct suspicion at any number of others, but certainly not at herself. How could a poor crippled woman be connected with anything so sinister, so sordid, so physically difficult?

And why did the hands actually have to be removed? Because they had been worn to the bone in Seton's frantic efforts to escape.

It's all devilishly clever but very, very contrived. It is hard to keep from coming back to the central question: how did Dalgleish know, when James has to use the device of a posthumous confession to make it clear to the rest of the world?

There is an explanation of sorts. After Digby's death, Dalgleish says to Reckless:

> "When I was in London yesterday it came to me how Maurice Seton could have been killed. It's little more than conjecture at present and God knows how you'll be able to prove it. But I think I know how it was done."
>
> Briefly he outlined his theory. . . .
>
> "What put you on to that, Mr. Dalgleish?"
>
> "I'm not altogether sure. A number of small things I suppose. The terms of Seton's will, the way he behaved at that basement table in the Cortez Club, his insistence on having one particular room whenever he stayed at the Cadaver Club, the architecture of his house even."

Still, prior to Sylvia's confession, there is no specific mention of claustrophobia. The steward at the Cadaver Club explains that Seton stayed on the first floor because "he hadn't any confidence in lifts." How Dalgleish makes the intuitive leap from this hint to a certain knowledge of claustrophobia is difficult to see.

But if the final denouement is somewhat unsatisfying, the book as a whole is not.

There are, first of all, so many eccentric characters. James is having a lot of fun at the expense of writers, and the reader is carried right along. It is a pleasure getting to know Aunt Jane, a strong, sensible woman, and a fitting relation for Adam. And the further growth of Dalgleish's own personality is fascinating.

But, most of all, there is Sylvia Kedge, perverted and sadistic, yes, but a haunting personality. Her description of the rage that she feels strikes hard, and lingers:

> "Adam Dalgleish. He can hardly bear to look at me. It's as if he's saying, 'I like women to be graceful. I'm sorry for you but you offend me.' I offend myself, Superintendent! I offend myself . . ."

The words ring on and on. "I offend myself!"—that is the epitaph of Sylvia Kedge. It is both her reason for the crime, and her excuse.

As for the final turn of the plot—that Sylvia, having committed the perfect crime, is swept to her death in a flood—it seems to tell a lot about James the writer, who writes about crime but does not admire criminals and cannot let them get away with their deeds. When the ordinary course of justice is not enough, she introduces an offstage retribution that makes sure a murderer does not go scot-free. It may not be "real life," but it's the way she prefers to tell her story. Crime does not pay.

It has been an exhausting "holiday" for Adam Dalgleish. There hasn't been much time for thoughts of Deborah Riscoe, only that one night when Adam poured his feelings into a poem expressing his need of her. But the poem, and the letter accompanying it, have not been mailed, for the storm intervenes and with it the searing events of Sylvia Kedge's rooftop. And then an envelope, in Deborah's hand, arrives for him. As soon as he sees it, he knows . . .

It is over. She has tired of waiting, has come to the realization that Adam Dalgleish belongs only to his work, no matter how he might protest that fact. She has accepted her firm's offer of a place on its American staff; she is on her way to New York.

Deborah knows Adam better, perhaps, than he knows himself, and she has made the right decision. And he, for all his momentary hurt, knows it, too. He takes both the letters, his and hers, and throws them on the fire.

The Deborah period is finished. For the next ten years, at least, Dalgleish will confine his emotional life to his poetry and let nothing, and no one, interfere with the proper execution of his job.

FOUR NOVELS
OF THE SEVENTIES
Shroud for a Nightingale
An Unsuitable Job for a Woman
The Black Tower
Death of an Expert Witness

P.D. James's second decade as a writer brought several major developments, not the least of which was the spread of her reputation and popularity across the Atlantic. American critics, who had all but ignored her first efforts, suddenly took notice of this modest British woman whose stories equaled and even surpassed the standards set by such famous figures as Sayers, Allingham and Tey. Meanwhile, three of her books won the Silver Dagger Award of the British Crime Writers' Association and one, *An Unsuitable Job for a Woman*, was a nominee for the Mystery Writers of America's Edgar Award. Certainly James—and Adam Dalgleish—had "arrived."

All four of the books of the seventies include her now-famous Scotland Yard detective although one, again, *An Unsuitable Job for a Woman*, concerns him only peripherally. An attractive new character surfaces in that book, Cordelia Gray, at twenty-two the sole proprietor of Pryde's Detective Agency.

Dalgleish, his thoughts of possible marriage to Deborah Riscoe behind him, grows older and advances in rank as the decade moves along. He even, for a time, toys with the idea of retiring, though in the end he does not, for his job is his life.

SHROUD FOR A NIGHTINGALE

The setting is institutional again, a hospital this time, and its nurse training school; James has returned to the scenes she knows best. Specifically, this novel takes place at Nightingale House, the nurses' school attached to the John Carpendar Hospital in Heatheringfield, at the Sussex-Hampshire border. It is a bleak, cold day in January, and the inspector of Nurse Training Schools, Miss Muriel Beale, has arrived for her annual visit. She is to watch the student nurses demonstrate, using each other as patients, the theories and techniques of intragastral feeding—that is, feeding directly into the stomach by means of a tube.

The demonstration never gets a chance to proceed very far, for seconds after the tube has been swallowed by Student Nurse Pearce and the drip of warm milk begun, the young "patient" lies gasping in agony on the floor, unresponsive to the ministrations of the assembled medical staff. She is dead within minutes—cruelly, horribly dead.

The milk in the feed had been replaced by carbolic acid, and Nurse Pearce has had her stomach burned away in what must surely be one of the more gruesome fictional murders of the decade.

At first no one will admit it is murder. It must have been a joke, it is explained, a stupid joke that backfired. Yet it is difficult to explain how a third-year nursing student—or any of the senior staff—could fail to realize what effect carbolic acid would have on the delicate lining of the stomach.

If it was murder, there is still a question of whether Pearce was really meant to be the victim. She had not been scheduled to act the part of patient that fateful day but had filled in only at the last moment when the scheduled student, Nurse Jo Fallon, had reported ill. There is conjecture that Fallon had been meant to die that dreadful death; it is one of the theories being investigated by the local C.I.D.

And then two weeks later murder strikes again, and this time it is indeed Fallon who is the victim. Someone has slipped poison—

nicotine, it is discovered later—into the whiskey and lemon night-cap that Fallon habitually carries up to bed with her each evening. Sometime during the night, silently and alone, Jo Fallon has died. Now there is no doubt; a murderer is loose at the John Carpendar. Dalgleish arrives to take charge of the investigation.

He is now a Chief Superintendent, and along with his new title he has brought a new assistant:

> Sergeant Charles Masterson was 6 feet 3 inches tall and broad-shouldered. He carried his bulk easily . . . for such an assertively masculine and heavy man. He was generally considered handsome, particularly by himself . . .

The two men are not overly fond of each other—Masterson, because he feels himself to be superior to his chief, despite the latter's far greater age and experience, and Dalgleish, because he senses a lack of deference on the part of the junior officer, deference that he knows is his due. They are two strong person-alities in a situation that has room for only one. But Masterson isn't stupid; he knows it would be folly to antagonize his superior. Dalgleish, for his part, is concerned only with results and will not let personal feelings interfere with the job at hand.

That job begins, as Dalgleish's investigations usually do, with the systematic interviewing of all those involved. In this case that means the other student nurses: twin sisters named Maureen and Shirley Burt, Julia Pardoe, Christine Dakers, Diane Harper, and Madeleine Goodale. And it means the staff: the Matron, Mary Taylor; Registered Nurses (Sisters) Brumfett, Rolfe, and Gearing; Gearing's lover, Pharmacist Len Morris; and a surgeon, Dr. Stephen Courtney-Briggs. Another student nurse left the school after the first murder and is never a suspect.

The first thing to emerge is that Heather Pearce, whether she was the intended victim or not, had a lot of enemies. She was a "self-righteous little beast" who had tried blackmail more than once. She spent most of her time prying into other people's private lives, looking for the one secret that they would not want spread about the school. Since nearly everyone has something, however small, to hide, Pearce was often successful in her quest. Half the girls and even some of the staff encountered her bullying tactics at one time or another, and not all were fortunate enough to be able to buy her off. No one is sorry about her death; more than one is actually glad.

Once again James has portrayed a victim who arouses no feelings of pity or remorse. In this case Pearce's personality is a necessary part of the plot—she "asked for" death, in a sense—but even when it is not necessary to the story, James makes an effort to create victims whose deaths are not really disturbing. Enid Bolam, for example (in *A Mind to Murder*) is murdered for money, not because she was an unlikeable person, although she was. One knows that, had she been warm and lovable instead of the stern, unbending person she was, her fate would not have been any different.

So it seems that personality, while not unimportant to the sequence of events, is not the factor that determines who is to die; therefore, if James's victims are all, or nearly all, unpleasant people, it must be because she prefers them to be so.

Nurse Pearce is true to this mold; Nurse Fallon, outwardly a much more attractive young woman, does not at first glance seem to be. She hasn't, apparently, any enemies, certainly no obvious ones at any rate. But neither has she any friends. She is, to be sure, some ten years old than her fellow students and, for that reason, would be expected to be somewhat apart from them, but she hasn't any friends outside of the hospital either. She has had several sexual liaisons that come to light, but she seems never to have been in love, nor to have been loved; she was as cool, detached, and unaffected by these relationships as she was by all the others in her life.

No one, Dalgleish decides, really knew Jo Fallon except Jo Fallon, and she kept her own counsel. So, while her death does not seem to bring relief to anyone, neither does it bring grief. She is still another victim about whom the reader will not feel sorrow, anger, or outrage.

The plot progresses slowly, but the various emerging personalities counteract the paucity of action. James is doing what she does so well, creating an entire stage-set, building a very real, very detailed world, brick by brick.

Institutional life is oppressive, particularly, it would seem, the nearly all-female life peculiar to such institutions as nurse-training schools. In its tight, rule-bound structure, the school is like a nunnery; the minds of its inhabitants (one almost wants to say inmates) are as rigid as its rules.

It is hard to believe there were ever such places as Nightingale House. But knowing James's hospital background, and her care in creating her settings, it is apparent that, in England at least, there were such places as late as 1971, when this book was published. The John Carpendar Hospital and its school are the old-fashioned, totally regimented institutions that one generally associates with the early years of this century, and the resident characters are modern people caught in a time-warp:

> She had given him a depressing glimpse into the stultifying lack of privacy, and of the small pettinesses and subterfuges with which people living in unwelcome proximity try to preserve their own privacy or invade that of others. . . . Small wonder that Nightingale House bred its own brand of neurosis, that Sister Gearing felt it necessary to justify a walk with her lover in the grounds, their obvious and natural wish to prolong the final good night, with unconvincing twaddle about the need to discuss hospital business. He found it all profoundly depressing and he wasn't sorry when it was time to let her go.

Clues come slowly. But finally, thanks to a confidence that Dalgleish elicits from the half-witted young cleaning woman, Morag Smith, the scope of the inquiry—at least that part of the inquiry dealing with the death of Heather Pearce—is dramatically narrowed. The place it leads to, without question, is the Resident Sisters' kitchen. It is now clear that is where the warm milk, the milk that was supposed to be used in the intragastral demonstration, had ended up. What is somewhat less clear is whether or not the bottle full of carbolic acid came from the same place.

Soon it is discovered that, several weeks before, a dying patient being nursed by Pearce had recognized one of the staff as a person who had stood trial at Nuremberg in 1946, accused of war crimes of a medical nature. Known at that time as Irmgard Groble, she had been acquitted, perhaps because of her youth, perhaps because she had actually been innocent. Afterwards she had made a new life in England and obviously would not want this piece of her past to come to light. That Pearce had acted on this knowledge for her own petty ends is clear; that act cost her her life. What is unclear is which woman, among the staff, is really Irmgard Groble.

There is no outward characteristic to give away her identity. The reference book on the War Crimes Trials, which figures heavily in the eventual denouement of the case, has no photograph of her, not that such a photograph would necessarily show much in any case, after such a span of years. And none of the Sisters in question has any trace of a German accent.

But before Groble's identity can be established—a task that would not have been difficult, once Dalgleish had time to probe into the backgrounds of the different characters—another twist occurs in the plot. The wooded grounds outside the hospital are the scene of a major nighttime fire. One of the casualties of that fire is a small storage hut sometimes used as a refuge by Morag Smith and, in that hut, burned almost beyond recognition, is the body of Sister Brumfett.

A quick check of her room by Matron Mary Taylor discloses an envelope containing a detailed confession of the two murders: "I killed Heather Pearce and Josephine Fallon. They had discovered something about my past, something which was no concern of theirs, and were threatening to blackmail me . . ."

It is all neatly laid out and explained. There is no question, because of the inclusion of details known only to the killer, that Brumfett was indeed that killer, however difficult it is for the reader to reconcile Brumfett's established character as a devoted, caring nurse with Pearce's gruesome death and Fallon's essentially unnecessary, though more "humane" one. There is no question, too, that the document is in Brumfett's own hand.

It is apparent, then, that in a frenzy of self-disgust, both at her own past and at her hand in these two recent deaths, Sister Brumfett has left her confession for all to see and has taken her own life by fire. The law will be satisfied; the reader, up to this point, is as well. But Adam Dalgleish is not satisfied; for him, this case is not over. He knows Brumfett's confession is the truth, but it is not the *whole* truth. It leaves a lot unsaid, and, although he knows, in fact, what really happened and why, he is powerless to prove it. The other person involved knows this full well. Part of this crime—these crimes—is, in fact, truly "perfect" and forever insoluble.

The murders of Pearce and Fallon are solved, and the murderer is dead. But Dalgleish knows there is one guilty party remaining free, and in his own mind the case is a festering wound, destined to be another one of his failures.

James refuses to make her hero omnipotent. Adam Dalgleish

comes across as a very real man, precisely because he has doubts and fears and, ultimately, failures—even if, as in this case, they are only failures of degree. Dalgleish is most emphatically not a "paper detective," perfect in every way. He is human. He even, in this book, finds himself strongly attracted to a murderer, even while he is repelled by her, and prepared to bring her to justice, if he possibly can.

He can't, but the story doesn't end there. It is unfortunate that it doesn't. James, after building a story of subtle complexity, after presenting a credible yet unexpected twist after Brumfett's death, after making Dalgleish still more memorable and believable because of his self-perceived failure, tacks on one of her drawn-out endings in which retribution is visited on the guilty by forces beyond the law. As she did in *Unnatural Causes*, where a violent storm swept the murderer to a watery death, and as she would do again in *An Unsuitable Job for a Woman*, she has fate step in to achieve what Dalgleish and the Law cannot accomplish. In this case it is conscience that is the driving force, Mary Taylor's conscience, which forces her to commit suicide in an essentially unbelievable way. The scales of justice are balanced, but one can't help thinking that the story would have been a better one had the scales been left somewhat awry.

Even Dalgleish, who should feel vindicated with this last turn of events, seems disappointed and unsatisfied. He holds the suicide note in his hand, proof at last of the crime he had known about all along, but he cannot bring himself to make it public. He would not have hesitated to bring Mary Taylor to justice if he had had it within his power to do so, but by taking her own life she has deprived him of any reason, except revenge, for so doing. Adam Dalgleish is not a vengeful man. He drops the note into the fire, and watches it slowly burn.

AN UNSUITABLE JOB FOR A WOMAN

Perhaps the most talked-about, and certainly the most unusual, of James's first seven novels is *An Unsuitable Job for a Woman*, published in 1972. For the first time Adam Dalgleish appears as only a secondary character, and the actual sleuthing is done by a new detective, Cordelia Gray.

Cordelia is only twenty-two and has fallen into her job almost by accident. After a highly unorthodox childhood—her mother dead, her father an adored "itinerant Marxist poet and amateur revolutionary," her education supervised by Roman Catholic nuns who eventually despaired of fitting Cordelia's free spirit into their mold—she had joined Bernie Pryde's newly formed detective agency as a sort of Girl Friday but was quickly made his partner. She may have had no direct investigative experience, but she has a keen intelligence, a strong young body, and an almost foolhardy absence of fear. Bernie knows the importance of these qualities; they are far more necessary than procedural details, which can be learned later. So Cordelia finds herself, at that early age, a private detective.

Then, before she has time to despair over their appalling lack of business, fate deals her another card. Arriving at the office one morning, she discovers Bernie's door locked, with him inside and a note from him on her desk:

"I'm sorry, partner, they've told me it's cancer and I'm taking the easy way out. I've seen what the treatment does to people and I'm not having any. . . . I've left the business to you. Everything . . ."

He had slit his wrists and bled to death. Cordelia's unsought legacy, she finds, is more shadow than substance; the business is on its last legs, with assets enough to keep it going for perhaps a few weeks at most. Nevertheless she determines to try. She has learned a lot from Bernie—maxims and rules of thumb enough to see her through many a crisis. And they are all pure gold—they came straight to Bernie from the lips of the great Adam Dalgleish.

For Bernie Pryde had once worked for the Metropolitan Police in the C.I.D with Superintendent—then Inspector—Dalgleish. His attitude toward his superior officer had been one of unadulterated hero worship, an attitude that was, unfortunately for Bernie, neither appreciated nor in fact even perceived by Dalgleish himself. That didn't matter. Bernie Pryde hung on the "Super's" every word, receiving each pronouncement like a gift and engraving it forever on his consciousness. He was a walking textbook of proper investigative procedures.

What he was not was a detective. Successful police work requires more than a rote memory; it requires imagination, inspiration, even flair. Bernie didn't have those qualities. Despite his attention to detail, despite even his overwhelming desire to do the job, Bernie Pryde failed. And if there is one thing that Adam Dalgleish will not tolerate in his department, it is failure.

There is only one factor that Dalgleish considers truly important in his job: results. In all his relationships with subordinates, the success of the investigation is the only thing he cares about; personal feelings, whether likes or dislikes, are irrelevant. He may acknowledge such feelings in himself, but he can successfully subordinate them to the job at hand. More often, he is unaware of them at all. He was certainly unaware, in Bernie's case, of the man's near-adoration of him, but he was very aware of the fact that Pryde was a failure as a policeman. He did the only thing he would ever do under the circumstances—he fired him.

It had shattered Bernie—he would ever after see himself as a failure, and in fact would be one—but it never changed his opinion of Dalgleish, who continued to personify all that was correct in police work. Nor did it change Bernie's lifelong desire to do the work he was obviously not cut out to do. Eventually he opened his own private-detective agency, lived by the rules he had memorized from the still-revered Dalgleish, and linked up with Cordelia Gray.

Then, undefeated in spirit despite a series of failures in fact, Bernie Pryde received the final blow, in the form of an inoperable cancer, and took his own life. His last wish was that Cordelia carry on his work.

First, however, she needs a case to work on. After days of sitting in an empty office, she gets one, when a Miss Leaming, representing her employer Sir Ronald Callendar of Cambridge, asks Pryde's Agency to investigate the circumstances surrounding the recent suicide of Callendar's only son, Mark.

It is a task made to order for Cordelia. She can easily blend into the college-age crowd at Cambridge and elicit information no "ordinary" detective could. She accepts, and the two women depart together, their destination, Garfort House, Sir Ronald's microbiology lab-cum-commune in Cambridgeshire, where he carries out the work for which he had won his fame and his title, assisted by a few reverent scientific aides and other laboratory staff. Cordelia had heard of him, "from his television appearances, and the Sunday supplements."

Callendar explains the specifics of the case:

> "My son Mark was 21 on the 25th April of this year. He was at Cambridge reading history ... and was in his final year. Five weeks ago and without warning, he left the University and took a job as a gardener with a Major Markland, who lives in a house called Summertrees outside Duxford. ... Eighteen days later he was found by his employer's sister hanging by the neck from a strap knotted to a hook in the sitting-room ceiling. The verdict of the inquest was that he took his life while the balance of his mind was disturbed. I know little of my son's mind but I reject that comfortable euphemism. ... He had a reason for his action. I want to know what it was."

It is a perfectly straightforward request from a man who is used to finding answers to specific problems, thinks Cordelia. She asks if Mark left a suicide note.

> "He left a note but not an explanation. It was found in his typewriter."
> Quietly Miss Leaming began to speak:
> "Down the winding cavern we groped our tedious way, till a void boundless as the nether sky appeared beneath us ..."

So, thinks Cordelia, he read Blake—fact number one: perhaps unimportant, perhaps not. "Get to know the dead person," the Super had taught.

She sets off for Duxford to meet Mark's last employers and is unexpectedly offered the use of the old gardener's cottage that Mark had lived in. It hasn't been touched since his death; dishes are set out for a meal never eaten, his pitchfork still stands in the little garden he had begun to plant outside the door. Upstairs Cordelia finds his clothes, his wallet, his Blake. Slowly, cautiously, she lets his personality seep into her subconscious, even as she clears a space for herself in his house. From here she will travel back and forth to Cambridge for the interviews she knows will be necessary.

She has one name to work on, the name of a former girlfriend of Mark's, Sophia Tilling. With remarkable ease—luckily, it's summer and the students spend most of their time outdoors—she runs into not only Sophia but also her brother Hugo, and two other of Mark's friends, Isabelle de Lasterie and Davie Stevens. These four knew Mark as well as anyone but profess to be just

as puzzled by his suicide as his father is: "Mark was a very private person. . . . He was quiet, gentle, self-contained . . ."
And Hugo adds, with anger:

> "He was sweet and he is dead. There you have it. . . . We none of us saw him after he chucked college. He didn't consult us before he left, and he didn't consult us before he killed himself. He was, as my sister has told you, a very private person. I suggest you leave him that privacy."

If Cordelia wonders why the four seem so vehement about this, she is careful not to say so. And despite their initial standoffishness, they quickly come to accept her, even to like her, as they include her in some typical summer amusements—punting on the Cam, partying, picnicking. The summer university life is beautifully portrayed by James, though one may wonder when anyone had time for studying.

> Afterwards, Cordelia remembered the river picnic as a series of brief but intensely clear pictures, moments in which sight and sense fused and time seemed momentarily arrested while the sunlit image was impressed on her mind. Sunlight sparkling on the river and gilding the hairs of Davie's chest . . . green-black weeds dragged by the pole from mysterious depths to writhe sinuously below the surface; a bright duck cocking its white tail before disappearing in a flurry of green water. When they had rocked under Silver Street Bridge a friend of Sophie's swam alongside, sleek and snout-nosed like an otter, his black hair laying like blades across his cheeks. He rested his hands on the punt and opened his mouth to be fed chunks of sandwiches by a protesting Sophie. The punts and canoes scraped and jostled each other in the turbulence of white water racing under the bridge. The air rang with laughing voices and the green banks were peopled with half-naked bodies lying supine with their faces to the sun . . .
>
> Here, rocking gently on the sunlit river, [thoughts of murder] seemed both indecent and absurd. She was in danger of being lulled into a gentle acceptance of defeat . . .

Two facts emerge that may be significant. On his twenty-first birthday, Mark had a visitor, an old woman who stayed with him for over an hour. A few weeks later, on his death, the largest array of flowers bore the card, "From Nanny Pilbeam." Whether these two are related, and what part Nanny Pilbeam had played in Mark Callendar's early life, are left to Cordelia to discover. She does, but not until she has unearthed the truth from Mark's four Cambridge friends about their where-abouts, and actions, on the night of his death.

Only three of them, not four, had gone to a play on that night as they'd originally claimed. Isabelle had gone to visit Mark. On her arrival she had found him—strung up on a hook by his belt, dressed in women's black underwear, his face rouged and painted in a caricature of sexual deviation. On a table nearby were pictures of naked women. He was, of course, dead.

She had, Isabelle reports, kept her head; she went back to Cambridge and told her friends, and together they decided to return to Mark's cottage, clean him up, and fake a suicide. It seemed obvious to them that he had died accidentally during an elaborate sexual charade, and they wanted to spare him, after that death, the inevitable scandal that would arise were the true conditions known. Hugo takes up the story:

> "We had no intention of letting the fuzz and Ronald Callendar know how Mark had died. . . . However, our good intentions were frustrated. Someone else had got here first.
>
> "We found . . . Mark naked except for his blue jeans. There were no magazines on the table and no lipstick on his face. But there was a suicide note in his typewriter.
>
> "Mark must have had more visitors that night than during his whole time at the cottage; first Isabelle, then the unknown Samaritan, then us."
>
> Cordelia thought that there had been someone before Isabelle. Mark's murderer . . .

Cordelia's investigations lead her to Somerset House, London, where she checks the conditions of Mark's grandfather's will—and finds that the age at which he would inherit his share of the old man's fortune was twenty-five, not twenty-one. Yet something happened on his twenty-first birthday, something that led to his leaving college and, ultimately, to his being murdered.

Some relentless legwork yields a dividend: Cordelia finds the florist from whom Nanny Pilbeam's flowers were ordered, and through the shop's order book is able to discover the woman's full name and address. However, before she can drive out to interview the woman, she has to fight off an attempt on her own life:

> If there were any more secret visitors she wanted to be warned.
> But the tape was still intact. . . . She wasn't expecting trouble outside
> the cottage and the attack took her completely by surprise. There
> was the half-second of pre-knowledge before the blanket fell but that
> was too late. There was a cord around her neck pulling the mask of
> hot stifling wool against her mouth and nostrils. Then a sharp pain
> exploded in her chest and she remembered nothing.

After this paragraph James throws Cordelia, literally and fig-
uratively, into a hell-on-earth. There is a struggle, then the
assailant whips the blanket off just as the young detective plummets
into a long-abandoned well. She awakens just in time to save
herself from drowning; the cold well water revives her, and she
treads water, blinking to clear both her eyes and her head. She
has seen no one and still does not know who her enemy is, but she
knows that it hardly matters unless she gets out of that well alive.

She does, thanks to her twenty-two-year-old muscles, a fierce
determination, and more than a little luck. It is not James's
strength to write scenes of physical tension, as it is to describe
psychological tension, and Cordelia's exploits seem just a bit
unbelievable. Technically, though, it is all possible, and eventually
she is safe above ground once again.

There are more adventures, even dangers, but Cordelia perse-
veres, and in the end learns the truth. She learns it, at last, from
Sir Ronald Callendar's own lips, and it is a sordid truth, indeed—
certainly to Cordelia herself, but even more so to Miss Leaming,
who overhears it and, on doing so, shoots the knighted scientist
and kills him with the unregistered gun Bernie Pryde had willed
to Cordelia.

A murderer, thinks Cordelia, deserves to die, and she cannot
condemn the woman who pulled the trigger. True justice has been
done with that act—and any further probe, any trial of Miss
Leaming, with its subsequent investigations, would help no one,
but only hurt the memory of the young man Cordelia has come
almost to love: Mark Callendar.

The two women conspire to make this death a suicide, a feat
which, because of Cordelia's training in criminology, they are able
to do. Her story is that she had just told Sir Ronald of her utter

failure in her quest and had asked to be released from her commission. He agreed to pay her the following morning, at which time he would return her gun, which he had kept for safety's sake while she worked for him. She was just leaving the house, saying goodby to Miss Leaming, when together they heard the shot . . .

No one can disprove her story. Cordelia Gray has successfully completed her first case by aiding a murderer to go free and declaring that her investigations in the matter of Mark Callendar had yielded nothing. All in the name of justice—abstract, not legal, justice, the concept, not the application of it.

Someone, however, knows the truth: Adam Dalgleish. That "supercilious, sapient, superhuman" Adam Dalgleish, whom she had heard quoted so often by Bernie Pryde that she thought he couldn't possibly be real, has heard about the case—Sir Ronald was a major figure, and couldn't be expected to pass away unnoticed—and found something there to ring untrue. He summons Cordelia to New Scotland Yard, and James records Cordelia's first impressions of him:

> The Superintendent she had pictured was very different from the tall austere figure who had risen to shake her hand. . . . He was old, of course, over forty at least, but not as old as she had expected. He was dark, very tall, and loose-limbed where she had expected him to be fair, thick-set and stocky. . . . His face was sensitive without being weak and . . . he sounded gentle and kind, which was cunning since she knew that he was dangerous and cruel.

At his questioning, she responds, "Why should I lie?" Dalgleish answers:

> "Well, it could be to protect yourself . . . or someone else. The motive for that could be love, fear, or a sense of justice. I don't think you've known any of the people in the case long enough to care for them deeply and . . . I don't think you would be easy to frighten. So we're left with Justice. A very dangerous concept, Miss Gray."

He knows. By determining her every move, and by discerning her reasons behind each move (which was easy—hadn't she learned it all from him?) he has, logically, arrived at the truth. To know, however, is not to prove; they are both aware of that.

Further confrontation is avoided, for James inserts at that point another act of retribution-outside-the-law. From Amalfi comes word of an accident. Miss Leaming has been killed when her car went out of control on the coast road . . . P.D. James cannot let crime go unpunished. If retribution does not come from the law, it will come from an outside force.

It is just another mild failure for Adam Dalgleish. Only he and Cordelia know the truth, and he will never be able to force it from her, he knows that. And now, with Miss Leaming dead, it is all academic anyway. In her acute relief, Cordelia confronts him with her pent-up rage against his treatment of Bernie Pryde:

> "And after you'd sacked him, you never even enquired how he got on. You didn't even come to the funeral."
>
> "I'm sorry . . . I didn't realize that your partner was the Bernie Pryde who once worked with me. It's rather worse than that, actually. I'd forgotten all about him."

Adam Dalgleish is cold, hard, distant, but Cordelia finds herself liking him (or admiring him, or respecting him) enough to want to see him again, though under circumstances less fraught with tension, circumstances in which he is not quite so in control. She makes the attempt, at least, in James's next book, *The Black Tower*.

An Unsuitable Job for a Woman is a departure for James in several respects. The most obvious, of course, is the use of a different central character and the relegation of Dalgleish to a secondary role. Another is the use of a wider scope than her previous "closed-community" stories. Here she depicts a science laboratory, but then quickly leaves it and its characters for the student world of Cambridge. To these two situations is added the shadowy world of Mark Callendar's boyhood—Nanny Pilbeam, an ancient doctor, even Mark's long-dead grandfather figure in the plot. There is no compact time frame and patient elimination of suspects as there has been in the Dalgleish novels. Cordelia's style is different (however much it is based on Dalgleish's principles), and so her settings must of necessity be different.

There is one other departure in this book. For the first time, in Mark Callendar, James has created a victim who is a thoroughly likeable person, one for whom the reader feels great pity and sorrow. He is dead not because of his own greed or because of flaws in his personality, but for precisely the opposite reasons. He is killed because he is an essentially honest person who cannot live a lie. The feelings that this arouses in Cordelia, and in the reader, too, give this novel greater dimension and depth than James's earlier works. She is even more firmly on the path of realism than she was before.

THE BLACK TOWER

As this book begins, Dalgleish has had a brush with death—not, as might be expected, in the course of his work, but from illness, an "atypical mononucleosis," which was not in itself serious but which mimicked the symptoms of a fatal leukemia. His physicians were fooled at first into the more pessimistic diagnosis, and Dalgleish, who is nothing if not perceptive, knew what they were fearing. He had progressed from anger to acceptance of his fate, when the final lab tests brought the happy news that his illness would run its own course and leave him, within a few weeks, weakened but essentially healthy.

Dalgleish's reaction to all this was as much anger as exultation, anger at his doctors who had let him believe the worst:

> It was, he thought, uncommonly inconsiderate if not negligent of his doctors to reconcile him so thoroughly to death and then change their minds. It was embarrassing now to recall with what little regret he had let slip his pleasures. . . . Now he had to lay hold of them again and believe that they were important, at least to himself.

He doesn't know what he ever again will consider important, so vastly has the specter of death changed his perspective, but he does know one thing. He will not return to "the whole bloody business of manhunting." He will resign from the Yard.

But first he has a few weeks of convalescence ahead of him, before he has to make that decision known. He'll use the time to read, write, think, and generally sort out the pieces of his life.

For the first time since he entered the hospital Dalgleish has the strength to look at his mail. There is a short note from Cordelia Gray, to accompany a bouquet of wildflowers she had picked (how like Cordelia to choose the perfect gesture), and he tells himself he will write her as soon as he can. There are other flowers, and dozens of cards. And there is a letter from an old priest, Father Baddeley, who had served as curate to Adam's father, a minister, some thirty years before.

The two men do not usually correspond, and the letter is unexpected. It is an invitation of sorts—really a summons for help. "I would very much welcome a visit from you as there is a matter on which I would be glad of your professional advice," writes the old man. Adam is intrigued and, remembering the priest with fondness, he is touched. He decides that a short stay with Father Baddeley would be ideal for his convalescence and writes to say he will arrive by car on October 1, less than two weeks away.

Father Baddeley is chaplain of Toynton Grange, a private home for the young disabled located in Dorset, on England's east coast. The Grange is a relatively small facility, more like an extended family than an institution, although its founder-warden, Wilfred Anstey, runs it like a monastery, with an inflexible daily schedule and ironclad rules by which all must live. Those patients able to work are kept busy manufacturing and distributing cosmetics bearing the Toynton Grange name. The small number of staff and patients assures that everyone is rather too close for comfort; privacy is minimal and tempers short. Trying to be the best of both worlds, family and institution, it has succeeded in becoming the worst.

When Dalgleish arrives, he discovers his host has died of a heart attack a few days before and has already been cremated. Of course no one has notified him; no one knew he was coming. However, the old man has left him his books, and Dalgleish must convalesce somewhere. He decides to stay on while he sorts out the library. Anstey assures him he is welcome to eat at the Grange and use the old priest's cottage for as long as he likes. So it is settled, and Dalgleish enters the bizarre world of Toynton Grange.

The people he encounters are a quirky lot. There is Anstey himself, so filled with religious zeal after a miraculous cure at Lourdes that he has dedicated his fortune and his life to helping other young disabled persons. Toynton Grange is the result of his charitable impulses, its religious overtones the result of his own Catholic conversion. He wears a monk's habit (and insists that most of the staff do the same) and takes the entire group on twice-yearly treks to the shrine where his own "miracle" occurred.

Anstey's sister Millicent is a rather acid-tongued hanger-on who is concerned, not surprisingly, with the way her brother is handling this very valuable estate of Toynton Grange in which she, as his next of kin, has a pecuniary interest.

The Hewsons, Maggie and Eric, share a private cottage on the grounds; Dr. Hewson is the resident physician. He is also, the reader learns, without a current license to practice, due to some indiscretion with a sixteen-year-old patient. His wife spends her time complaining about their present situation and daydreaming of better things.

There is, it seems, a little something awry in the lives of most of the staff. Dot Moxon, the very capable Matron, was investigated on a cruelty charge at her last hospital job. Philby, who does odd jobs, is an ex-convict. Dennis Lerner, the male nurse, has too strong an attachment to one of the male patients. The female nurse, Helen Rainer, is carrying on a not-very-secret affair with Dr. Hewson. All of them seem, to Dalgleish, to be unhappy, bitter, and dissatisfied, both with themselves and with Toynton Grange.

The bitterness extends, as well, to the patients, although in their cases it is perhaps more understandable. They are all suffering from incurable, progressive diseases, and, while their symptoms and the degree of their incapacity varies from one to another, they are all unable to take care of themselves. This is not a condition to which any formerly healthy person easily adapts himself and may be particularly difficult for the young. (By "young," Wilfred Anstey means "not old"—his patients range from youth through middle age.)

There are only a few patients. Georgie Allan is the youngest and the most severely ill; he can barely sit up. Grace Willison is the oldest, gray-haired, with little strength. Jennie Pegram, a blond teenager just on the verge of adulthood, and Ursula Holliss, in her mid-twenties, are the other women.

Henry Carwadine is the only adult male patient, Dalgleish discovers, since Victor Holroyd threw himself to his death over the cliffs a few weeks before. Each of these patients is beset with fears, many of which have already come to pass: loss of love, of power, of money; loss of physical function and, equally important, physical attractiveness; loss of purpose; loss of control.

Seeing them gathered in their wheelchairs for tea, Dr. Hewson has a grotesque, sudden image of them all as puppets:

> Dr. Hewson had a momentary and insane picture of himself rushing

on to the patio and setting the four heads nodding and wagging, pulling invisible strings at the back of their necks.

It is a macabre scene, James trying out some black humor. She understands how the chronically ill or disabled can, simply by existing, make the rest of the world slightly uncomfortable, as if ashamed at its own good fortune. Eric Hewson does not wish evil on any of them, but he sees them, with their unresponsive muscles and powerless limbs, as something less than fully human. They are no longer in charge of themselves. Therefore, they are puppets—someone else is pulling the strings. The patients have good reason for their bitterness toward life.

All the staff members, for their various reasons, and all the patients not only take their daily dose of life as a bitter pill, they are all further burdened by the guilt they feel for their inability to be thankful to Wilfred Anstey for bringing them to this place. By his actions and through his rigid structuring of life at the Grange, he is saying, "Be grateful! Be glad you are here in this lovely place!" But he fails to realize that not one of them, except himself, really wants to be there. It is at best a refuge from the worse fate that would await them in the world. In truth it is a prison of sorts, one that they all fear they will never leave.

Into this world comes Adam Dalgleish, newly reacquainted with health and life, looking for a quiet convalescence and a new direction for his own future. Instead of either, he finds a maelstrom of death, drugs, and disordered minds. It is in no way the pleasant interval he expected when he first drove onto the grounds and marveled at the sight and sound of the sea. It is, in that sense, hardly the proper atmosphere for one newly risen from a hospital bed. Yet in another sense it is just what Adam Dalgleish needs. Involvement helps to bring him back to health.

The deaths seem unrelated at first; they just happen. One night without any warning and with no apparent motive, Grace Willison is strangled in her bed. Not long after, Maggie Hewson is found dead in her cottage, a suicide note at her feet. These two, added to the earlier deaths of Father Baddeley and Victor Holroyd, cannot possibly be coincidental, thinks Dalgleish. But he is an awkward situation; as in *Unnatural Causes*, he finds himself working "without portfolio," in an unofficial capacity. In that case he actually had to fight the antagonism of the local police officer, while in this he maintains friendly relations with the local force but still faces the stone wall of their disbelief. There have been four deaths, but except for that of Miss Willison there appears to have been no crime. Two suicides and a heart attack don't need police investigation.

Dalgleish thinks they do. He turns up a lot of interesting information on his own: That Wilfred Anstey's "miracle" was a hoax; the man never had the terminal illness of which he is supposed to have been cured. That Victor Holroyd, a spiteful, nasty man who liked nothing better than to discredit others, had somehow found this out. That Holroyd had also been responsible for the discovery and disruption of a homosexual relationship between Henry Carwadine and a young male patient, since transferred to another institution, a year before. That Grace Willison was the only person who knew the names of the Grange's patrons, those who bought the cosmetics made by the patients and who received a bimonthly newsletter. That Father Baddeley had been to the Black Tower, a circular building at the edge of the cliff, on the day Victor Holroyd died. That Julius Court, the only private citizen living on the grounds of the Grange, has tastes far beyond his means.

The clues are dropped thickly, but the meaning of them seems quite unclear, until Dalgleish has another of his famous hunches and brings light to the dark puzzle. He adds expensive tastes, mailing lists, cosmetics, and regular trips to France together and comes up with—drugs.

Someone is using the Grange's pilgrimages as a foil for drug smuggling and then, in a further step, is using the cosmetic sales as a distribution device. Suddenly some of the residents saw and heard things that would threaten this operation in one way or another; hence, the murders. For they all were indeed murders, Dalgleish knows. He has not yet found the proof he needs, but he will, he is certain.

Before he can, fate intervenes. It is the last morning of his visit, the morning when the Grange pilgrimage leaves for France. After they have gone, Dalgleish lingers, working out his theory, and is confronted by Julius Court, the only person who, he had decided, could have been the mastermind of the drug ring. Julius knows the game is up and pulls a gun—the prelude to a long and detailed confession, confirming Dalgleish's theories completely. But Court has the gun, Adam Dalgleish only his wits. Even his body, still weak from his illness, isn't an asset in this contest.

James is not at her best in descriptions of physical conflict, and nowhere is this more true than in the final scenes of this book. Of course the detective survives, and of course Julius Court doesn't; he falls to his death over the cliff edge, in his final hand-to-hand battle with Dalgleish after the gun has been dropped. But the events leading up to this, particularly the very chancy way Dalgleish manages to lead rescuers to himself just in time, strains credulity a great deal.

If the tumult of the ending is out of character for James, the bare facts of it aren't. That is, Court has to die in the way he did, since his involvement in the deaths would probably be impossible to prove. Once again James has the plot punish the true murderer, the really guilty, when Dalgleish and the law cannot.

Critics have called this book "melodramatic," and in the eyes of some it is James's weakest story. Certainly it is hard to believe in a health institution where the staff, male and female, all wear monks' habits. That is an obvious device used to obscure identity, and it is unsettling. The plot is overly complex and essentially unreal. But there is much more to this book than its plot. Despite its weaknesses, *The Black Tower* does stand on its own in the final analysis.

One strength is the different face of Dalgleish that James allows the reader to see in the first chapter. His thoughts while in the hospital, his musings in regard to life and death, add further dimension to his character.

Then there are the patients, with their bodies and personalities so horribly twisted with disease. James makes it obvious, as she did in the character of Sylvia Kedge in *Unnatural Causes*, that illness affects not only the body but also, in many cases, the mind of the afflicted. Small quirks of behavior can become enlarged out of all proportion when they are housed in an unsound body. But even as the reader recoils in horror from the perversity described at Toynton Grange, he will feel too a glimmer of understanding for it, and a sympathy for those who are trapped in unresponsive or even grotesque bodies. This is a recurring theme of James's, used to some degree in most of her stories, but developed most fully in Sylvia Kedge and in the inhabitants of Toynton Grange.

Cordelia Gray, mentioned in the first chapter with her gift of wildflowers, does not reappear either in the text or (apparently) in Adam's thoughts until the very last pages, when in his delirium following the cliff-edge fight, he murmurs her name. He is, however, old enough to be her father, and one suspects that he knows it. She does not appear at all in his next adventure, *Death of an Expert Witness*.

The Black Tower is a throwback, in one way, to James's earlier stories in that, once again, she uses a closed-community situation, and Toynton Grange, with its small number of inhabitants, is a textbook example. Yet in the end the murders are laid to the one resident who has regular contact with the outside world, and they also are tied to an international operation, the drug ring. James has taken a classic situation and adapted it to her own purposes.

DEATH OF AN EXPERT WITNESS

Medically oriented people and places continue to play a part in this last of James's 1970s novels, but they are deftly interwoven into a background of police work, as the author sets her scene in a forensic science laboratory. Here pathologists, biologists, and other scientific specialists perform the various painstaking tests that establish much of the evidence in criminal proceedings.

Hoggatt's is a small independent laboratory located in the town of Chevisham in East Anglia. Remote from population centers and run by a staff of less than a dozen, it serves very well as the focus of another closed-community situation.

A murder begins the story, but not the murder with which the book is principally concerned; this first crime serves only to introduce the people and the lab. Murder is their business, and this one, called the Clunch Pit Murder, sets in motion the various processes by which the characters are defined. In the end, this crime is solved, and its discovery and solution act like a pair of bookends, on either side of the main story in the book.

The first to respond to the Clunch Pit Murder is the medical examiner, Doctor Kerrison. Recently divorced, he is a man with failed expectations and little sense of self-worth, but he does his job well and hopes for the recommendations that will change it from its present temporary status to a permanent one. Kerrison's preoccupation is in retaining custody of his children, sixteen-year-old Nell and five-year-old William. The fear that it is really only the little boy whom he cares about has turned Nell into a neurotic, pathetic figure, one who is tormenting her father and herself at the same time. James makes clear very early on that Nell would do anything to obtain her father's love, and that her warped emotions have blinded her, in many cases, to reality.

Maxim Howarth, newly appointed director of the lab, is also at the murder scene. There had been some opposition to his appointment, and he is trying to impress his immediate subordinates, that they might better accept him. One of them, Dr. Lorrimer, will never accept him, he knows; Lorrimer had wanted the job himself and continues to think himself by far the better qualified man. He'd taken his revenge, however, in a unique way, by becoming the lover of Howarth's widowed sister Domenica Schofield. Howarth, protective and almost unnaturally attached to his sister—they live together—will never forgive Lorrimer for that, though the affair has since ended.

Their work at the scene of the crime finished, the three men, with Inspector Doyle of the local police, return to the lab, where the rest of the staff is assembling for its working day. Included are Paul Middlemass, the document examiner; Clifford Bradley, higher scientific officer; Brenda Pridmore, receptionist; Inspector Blakelock of the police; Angela Foley, secretary; and Claire Easterbrook, senior scientific officer. Each is introduced separately as they leave for or arrive at work, and each, it is apparent, has some kind of personal problem. Most of these problems, in one way or another, involve one person—Edwin Lorrimer. Only Brenda Pridmore feels anything but distaste for the man; she likes him, but most of the rest fear him, or hate him, or both.

Then, shortly after, Edwin Lorrimer is murdered in his office, his skull smashed by a heavy mallet he had been examining. The doors were locked from the inside, indicating that the victim had let his killer in himself as he worked alone, as was his habit, in the evening. How that killer got out again is not immediately apparent.

It is a case for Scotland Yard. Dalgleish arrives at the remote site by helicopter, accompanied by one of the most interesting assistants he has had to date, Detective Inspector, The Honorable John Massingham:

> Dalgleish glanced at his companion, at the strong pale face, the spatter of freckles over the craggy nose and wide forehead, and the thatch of red hair . . . and thought how like the boy was to his father, that redoubtable, thrice-decorated peer, whose courage was equalled only by his obstinacy and naivete.

Still, Dalgleish goes on to think, "the police were a tolerant body and took the view that a man couldn't help who his father was. . . . They called Massingham The Honjohn behind his back, and occasionally to his face, and bore no malice."

Massingham is intelligent and earned his recent promotion on merit and not because he is the eldest son of a peer. Dalgleish likes working with him because he is both capable and sensitive. However, Dalgleish "had also been struck by a streak of ruthlessness in the boy which, he thought, ought not to have surprised him since he knew that, as with all good detectives, it must be present."

The two detectives are met by Dr. Howarth and given a tour of the laboratory. In her usual way, James describes the building, its architecture, layout, furnishings and functions with a thoroughness that bespeaks total familiarity with her subject. And in the matter of small, inventive detail, she can be amusing:

> But the most bizarre objects in the room were a pair of unclothed window-dresser's dummies, one male and one female, standing between the windows. They were unclothed and denuded of their wigs. . . .
> Howarth stared at the dummies as if he had never seen them before. He seemed to think that they required explanation. For the first time he had lost some of his assurance. He said:
> "That's Liz and Burton. The staff dress them up in a suspect's clothes so that they can match up bloodstains or slashes."

After the general inspection comes the interviewing. Dalgleish, as he does on every case, will attempt to get inside each of the suspect's personalities, to learn the *why* of their behavior even as he documents the factual details of movement and time. A violent act like murder doesn't just happen; it grows out of existing prejudices, hatreds, or fears. Discovering these hidden feelings is as much a part of Dalgleish's job as verifying an alibi, and he uses every method at his disposal including—or perhaps particularly— that of getting people to talk about each other.

Not for the first time James uses the device of the percipient cleaning woman as the see-all and know-all of her closed community. In *A Mind to Murder*, Mrs. Shorthouse is a well-meaning, gossipy woman without whose aid Dalgleish would have had a difficult time filling in background. Morag Smith, the semi-retarded housekeeper in *Shroud for a Nightingale*, in the end provides the key information leading to the killer. And now, in *Death of an Expert Witness*, James introduces Mrs. Bidwell, unlettered but shrewd, a keen judge of character and a woman whose powers of observation would rival those of a private eye.

What all three of these characters share is a total honesty, an upright morality that they wear like a signboard, and which is obvious at once to the reader and to Dalgleish. Their very status as subservient beings sets them aside at once from the list of suspects; they aren't even seriously investigated, except insofar as they are drawn to comment on the actions, habits, and personalities of the others. They act as a kind of counterpoint to the deadly serious action in which Dalgleish is engaged, and, while none of them is a comic character, each of them lightens the tone of the story in which she appears.

Through the stories of the various staff members and their families, the personality of Edwin Lorrimer emerges. Again, as in most of James's earlier books, the victim is portrayed as an unsympathetic character. Lorrimer was cold, cruel, demanding. That he demanded as much of himself as of others does not emerge as a virtue. He was methodically breaking the spirit of one of his subordinates, Clifford Bradley, a man of little talent, but one who, with praise, would have proved competent and loyal. Instead he was on the verge of a nervous breakdown because Lorrimer berated him, publicly and privately, over what he perceived to be minor errors of judgment. It never occurred to Lorrimer that his method of dealing with Bradley might be wrong.

> He said to me, "You're a third-rate biologist and a fourth-rate forensic scientist. That's what you were when you came into this

department and you'll never change. I have two alternatives, to check every one of your results or to risk the Service and this laboratory being discredited in court. Neither is tolerable. So I suggest that you look for another job. And now I've things to do so please leave."

Angela Foley is Lorrimer's cousin, but she feels no love for him either. They have never been close, and in recent years had been politely distant. Angela, a product of a broken marriage and a series of foster homes, has finally, as an adult, found the love she was denied as a child. But she has found it, much to Lorrimer's disgust, with another woman, a writer, Stella Mawson. The two women share a cottage and an apparently satisfactory relationship, but are pressed for money. Lorrimer is wealthy. He has recently changed his will specifically to exclude his cousin Angela—a fact of which she and Stella are unaware.

Dr. Howarth hates Lorrimer because of the man's affair with Howarth's sister Domenica. Howarth is rather too attached to Dom, as he calls her; they have a cozy relationship that borders on the incestuous, and which has become all the warmer since she broke off with Lorrimer. Why she felt the need for that affair in the first place is never totally explained, but it wasn't love, at least not on Domenica's part, for she loved only her brother—and herself. Lust may have explained it, or more accurately, the sexual thrill of power, of domination. Domenica is attractive, accomplished, and intelligent, and men are drawn to her, sometimes against their better judgment. Some, like Lorrimer, think what they feel is love. Domenica plays with such feelings as one would play with cards, or dominoes.

Whatever the truth behind her affair with Lorrimer, she knew well enough how it would affect her brother, and so kept it secret from him. He would never have known had not Lorrimer blurted it out to him, after it was finished, in a rage against Howarth, who had the only two things Lorrimer wanted—the directorship of the lab, and the love of Domenica. Howarth, meanwhile, could not help hating Lorrimer for having shared Domenica's bed, and for arousing feelings that he, as her brother, had never fully admitted even to himself.

Only Domenica emerges from that encounter unscathed; she seems to glide through life without touching it, while sending out vibrations that shatter other people as she passes by.

Nell Kerrison hated Lorrimer, too. She hated him indirectly, for having something to do with the telephone calls that drew her father away from home in the night to the scene of a murder, leaving her behind. Somehow, in her tortured mind, she equated that leaving with abandonment, as her mother had abandoned them all a year before, going away with her lover. Nell hated Lorrimer directly as well. He had angrily ejected her and her brother William from the lab a few days before, when they had gone there to wait for their father. He had really been unnecessarily cruel then: "He stared at us if he hated us, his face white and twitching . . ." Kerrison, when he discovered what Lorrimer had done, was furious in his daughter's behalf.

Painstakingly, Dalgleish and Massingham check alibis, track down clues, establish the time and truth of telephone calls. Routine police work, routinely done, establishes the time of death as between 8:45 and 9:11 P.M. It is a short span, but for a number of possible suspects, who have been unable to prove their whereabouts, it remains a very long period.

While Dalgleish is still sifting his thoughts and waiting for that one piece of incontrovertible evidence, Stella Mawson is hiding both background information and a temporarily unidentified paper she took from Lorrimer's room shortly after his death. She plans to act alone and doesn't even take Angela into her confidence, let alone Adam Dalgleish. She needs money and sees a way out— not blackmail, only a loan. However, a person who has killed once does not take kindly to extortion, even when it is cushioned by soft words and undemanding phrases. When Stella leaves the cottage to keep an appointment on the night after Lorrimer's murder, she is going to meet her own death.

In what is one of James's best scenes of eerie terror, little Brenda Pridmore discovers Stella's body hanging from a hook high on the wall of the Wren chapel just beyond Hoggatt's Lab.

Brenda, clearly an innocent, had discovered Lorrimer's body, too, but that was nothing compared to this—her panic is palpable, real. James has not always done this kind of scene well but this time she has succeeded admirably.

> And then she heard the noise, gentle as a single footfall, soft as the brush of a coat sleeve against wood. He was coming. He was here. . . .
> Sobbing, she threw herself from side to side against the walls,

thudding her bruised palms against the gritty, unyielding brick. Suddenly there was a space . . . then terror swooped with a wild screech of exultation and a thrashing of wings which lifted the hair from her scalp . . .

It is only at this point, after her death, that Stella Mawson's secret emerges, that once, many years before and in another place, she had been Lorrimer's wife. Their marriage, unconsummated after two years, was eventually annulled, and they had played the part of total strangers ever since. More than anyone else, Stella knew the truth of Lorrimer's nasty, compulsive, malicious character, and she truly hated him, both for the events of that failed marriage and for his contemptuous disregard of his cousin Angela. Rummaging in his desk after his murder, before the arrival of the police, Stella had found a draft letter written by Lorrimer containing information that might have been of use to the investigation. But, seeing the subject of that vicious letter as a fellow victim instead of as a potential murderer, she pocketed the evidence and told no one about it. Now she had attempted to use it to obtain the money she and Angela so badly needed, money to save their cottage from being sold. Instead she met death.

Lorrimer's other "victim" was Dr. Kerrison—the same man who, as medical examiner, was first to examine the body and who then had the opportunity to return to Lorrimer's pockets the keys that had figured largely in the investigation. Kerrison, who was struggling to retain custody of his children in the pending divorce, had also been in recent months Domenica Schofield's new lover, Lorrimer's "replacement." Lorrimer had just found out and had called him to the lab to threaten him, to tell him that he intended to write to Kerrison's wife with details of the present affair, details that would be very messy when aired in court. In a panic, Kerrison grabbed the mallet and struck his blackmailer a fatal blow. Then the following night when Stella Mawson offered to return the incriminating letter—Lorrimer's draft to Mrs. Kerrison—for a mere loan of £4000, he killed again. He didn't trust her to remain quiet, and he was determined that nothing must occur that would take the children from him.

By a long and devious route, Dalgleish has figured out the identity of the killer before James makes it clear; he has done so by discovering the Kerrison–Domenica Schofield connection and

Four Novels of the Seventies   57

the fact of their secret meetings in the Wren chapel. But he knows that it may be impossible to get the evidence that will prove his case. Kerrison says he was home during the crucial hours, and there is no one to dispute that fact. Indeed, telephone calls at 9:00 and 10:00 P.M. that evening seem to confirm it. Nell may know differently, but she will never admit it.

Yet in the end she does, and she does so as a result of Detective Massingham's "streak of ruthlessness," now made very evident. In a scene including the two policemen, Nell and William Kerrison, Miss Willard, their slatternly housekeeper, and Domenica Schofield, Miss Willard sets the stage. Screaming at Nell, she says:

> "It's William he loves, not you. I've seen his face, I've heard him, and I know. He's thinking of letting you go to your mother. You didn't know that, did you? And there's something else you don't know. What do you think your precious daddy is up to when he's drugged you to sleep? He sneaks off to the Wren chapel and makes love to her."

"Her" is Domenica Schofield. Nell doesn't believe it, and begs Dalgleish,

> "She's lying! Tell me she's lying! It isn't true."
> There was a silence. It could only have lasted a couple of seconds while Dalgleish's mind phrased the careful answer. Then, as if inpatient to forestall him, not looking at his chief's face, Massingham said clearly,
> "Yes, it's true."

So fragile Nell, whose only hope for sanity lay in eventually believing in her father's love, becomes the means by which the police are able to prove his guilt in two murders, and thereby destroys her own last chance for happiness. She is goaded into it partly by the spiteful Miss Willard, but principally by those three words of Massingham: "Yes, it's true." There is no spite behind his statement, only the need to do his job, which is to arrest the murderer. If innocent people are hurt thereby, it is an unavoidable side effect. Murder has many victims.

Massingham takes no pleasure in the pain he has caused; in fact, he is full of compassion for Nell. But he doesn't regret what he did. If he had been less blunt, she might not have told the truth, and the truth is what his whole investigation is about.

Dalgleish "wished never to see Massingham again." Yet he is conscious of the fact that, but for his assistant's words, he might have had to destroy Nell himself. He had been trying to frame an answer when Massingham spoke. He isn't sure that answer would have been very different.

> What Massingham had done seemed to him now unforgivable. But life had taught him that the unforgivable was usually the most easily forgiven. It was possible to do police work honestly; there was, indeed, no other safe way to do it. But it wasn't possible to do it without giving pain.

This portrayal of the pain caused by crime, not only to the victim and, eventually, to the criminal, but also to many innocent bystanders, is a major James theme, and nowhere has she enunciated it more clearly than she does in this book. Massingham and Dalgleish are not the only ones who feel Nell's pain; the reader feels it too. Nell has been shattered, in truth, not by Massingham's words but by the acts of the father she loved so much, and who committed the crime out of love for her.

It is a tragic story of desperate acts done by desperate people. What is accomplished is the polar opposite of what was intended. Kerrison will lose the children he wanted so to keep; Nell and William will lose the father they needed so badly.

One can almost feel sorry for the killer in this book, more so than in most of James's stories. Kerrison is wronged by his wife, disturbed by his daughter's emotional problems, bewitched by Domenica, goaded by Lorrimer, frightened by Stella Mawson. He isn't a bad man, but he reached the end of his rope and reacted with violence. As much as any character James has created, Kerrison represents the ordinary man pushed beyond his limits into the ultimate crime. Julius Court and Marion Bolam were greedy. Mrs. Maxie was proud, Mary Taylor cold-blooded, Sylvia Kedge vengeful, but Kerrison was afraid.

For the first time James has left two genuinely pathetic characters in bad straits at the finish. Nell Kerrison is broken by the discovery that her father had been seeing Domenica secretly. In her grief she blurts out the truth that will convict him of murder. She not only will have to live without him in the future, she'll have to live with the knowledge that she betrayed him, and in her fragile mental state, she may not be able to bear this burden. And Angela Foley, whose only happiness lay in serving and loving Stella Mawson, has lost Stella. She won't soon find someone else to give her the stability she is in need of. Neither Angela nor Nell deserves her fate, but each is left, at the conclusion of this story, to cope with it as well as she can.

In the opposite vein, Domenica Schofield emerges unscathed from a fray in which she was the original moving force. Domenica is one of those people who will always land on her feet and, since she will never really be "guilty" of anything, she will forever escape punishment.

Death of an Expert Witness represents a summit for P.D. James. Everything she had done well for twenty years, she did even better in this book. It is no coincidence that for her next effort, she chose to write in a different genre entirely.

4

INTO THE EIGHTIES
Innocent Blood

Over a period of two decades P.D. James refined her craft until she achieved, in *Death of an Expert Witness*, a kind of merger between the police procedural and the full-fledged novel. It was only a matter of time before she would divorce herself from the narrow field of the detective story entirely and plunge into the mainstream of popular fiction. In 1980, with the publication of *Innocent Blood*, she did just that—and met with almost overwhelming critical acclaim.

She did it, moreover, without changing the essentials of her writing style and without abandoning her major area of interest, crime. *Innocent Blood*, while not a mystery, is certainly a story of suspense, and deals with both past murder, and one that is about to take place. Whether it will—and under what circumstances—is one of the main elements in the plot.

The story begins when Phillippa Palfrey, adopted daughter of Maurice and Hilda Palfrey of London, reaches her eighteenth birthday and decides to exercise her right under the Children's Act of 1975 to discover the identity of her biological parents. She has woven a few fantasies about them—she's convinced she's the illegitimate daughter of a nobleman—but doesn't want to live the rest of her life with only an imaginary background. She wants a real identity, whatever the truth of it may be.

The social worker with whom she is obliged to consult warns her that "We all need our fantasies in order to live. Sometimes relinquishing them can be extraordinarily painful, not a rebirth into something exciting but a kind of death."

But Phillippa is undeterred; she wants the truth. When it comes, however, she isn't quite prepared for the enormity of it. Her parents, she discovers, are Martin and Mary Ducton, who were, in 1968, convicted of respectively raping and murdering a twelve-year-old girl named Julie Scase. Martin Ducton died a year later in prison, but his wife, having served ten years of a life sentence, is about to be paroled.

After an angry scene with her adoptive parents, with whom she has lived a physically comfortable but emotionally barren life, Phillippa decides that she will invite her mother to live with her in London for several months, until the time comes for Phillippa to go up to Cambridge to begin her university studies. Mary Ducton accepts, and mother and daughter begin the slow and painful process of establishing a relationship.

Someone else, however, is interested in Mary Ducton, too. Norman Scase, the fifty-seven-year-old father of the dead Julie, has paid a private detective to keep track of her during her imprisonment. He has made a deathbed vow to his wife, Mavis, to track her down and kill her upon her release. Now that release is imminent, and Norman Scase resigns from his job, sells his house and furniture, and devotes himself to the singular task he has undertaken.

The contrast between the almost make-believe, out-of-reality life being led by Phillippa and her mother, in a tiny flat above a grocery store in one of London's working-class neighborhoods, and the deadly serious tracking and stalking of them by Norman Scase is the heart of this novel. The parallel lines of the story—the slowly developing relationship between the two women, the care-fully formulated and executed plans of Scase—create a tension that is almost palpable in its intensity, a tension that builds to an inevitable climax and then, in true P.D. James style, spins out slowly to its neatly wrapped end.

The search for self and the human need for revenge and retribution are the main themes of this novel. Phillippa believes that only by finding her mother can she find herself, and in a sense she is right, though not for the reasons she imagines. When the book begins, she is a person estranged from the world. She has been given a comfortable home, an excellent education, material possessions both fine and expensive; she accepted it all as her due. Whatever love has been offered her by Hilda, her adoptive mother, she has rejected; she lives with, but apart from, the Palfreys and cares for no one at all. There is no question, in fact, that, when she decides to make contact with her mother, she takes pleasure in the fact that this action will hurt the people who adopted her ten years before.

Phillippa knows and appreciates good food, good wine, good literature and art, yet even in these things she finds little real pleasure; they are only amusing ways to pass the time in what is essentially a boring life. She wants to be a writer but, lacking any true emotional involvement with other people, does not know what to write about. She is very old for an eighteen-year-old, with none of the happy enthusiasm of youth, no optimism, no sense of fun.

Her adoptive father, Maurice Palfrey, is a popular sociologist, a teacher and author of many books, a frequent talk-show guest. He is urbane, eloquent, unswervingly sure of himself, and condescending to those who disagree with his theories. He has made Phillippa in his own image, sharpened her mind, molded her tastes to match his own; she suspects that he did it all, not from love, but as a sociological experiment. Subconsciously aware that she owes much of her personality to him, she rejects this knowledge, affecting to hate him because she can't bring herself to love him. This inability to face her real feelings for Maurice is a major reason why she feels compelled to seek her identity through biological ties rather than through environmental ones.

Towards Hilda, Maurice's wife, Phillippa has no feelings at all except pity and guilt. Pity, because Hilda is so inadequate according to the standards Maurice has set (and Phillippa has reached); guilt, because despite her inadequacies Hilda has tried and deserves something more than the contempt which is all that Maurice and Phillippa give her.

Phillippa seems not to have any friends, nor does she have a boyfriend in the usual sense, although she toys with a young aristocrat, the Honorable Gabriel Lomas, with whom she has had one (unsuccessful) sexual encounter. Gabriel is a good match for Phillippa; he is rich, amusing, and selfish, and so is she. She doesn't really like him but finds him handy to have around: "He was high on the list of objects of use and beauty which she planned to take with her to Cambridge."

Mary Ducton is not what one would expect, given the fact that she is a convicted child-killer. Her characterization, in fact, is the only thing that does not ring true in this book, and it is the novel's major flaw. She is not believable. In the words of one reviewer, Mary Ducton "even after spending ten years in jail sounds as if she's about to take her orals in English literature."

James, of course, is an extremely polished and literate writer whose principal characters are almost always educated and intelligent people who think and speak as well as their creator. Literary allusions and artistic references are sprinkled through their conversation with complete assurance that they will be both accepted and understood. Phillippa and her adoptive father fit this pattern; even Hilda, incompetent though she is supposed to be, can hold her own in conversation and not seem out of place. But when Mary Ducton starts discussing *Hamlet* or the novels of George Eliot something seems wrong.

Nor is this initial impression changed when details of Mary Ducton's background become clear. Abused by her father, she grew up with hidden terrors that later caused her to kill the child her husband had raped. She was clever, quick, intelligent, but uneducated, and, finding no satisfaction in her own life, could not cope with the demands made upon her by the birth of her child. That child—Phillippa, called Rose by her parents—was difficult, distant, and rejecting of love even as an infant, and the young mother was soon abusing her as she herself had been abused—a classic pattern. All this is understandable as explanation for both the crime and for Phillippa's own basic intelligence, but it doesn't explain how, after being convicted of murder and placed in prison with the worst of companions, this unlettered woman became the almost scholarly person she appears to be upon her release.

For Phillippa, her mother is a rough gem, needing only a few months' polishing by a firm and knowing hand in order to sparkle forever after. Phillippa will be that firm hand. Together they go about London, an odd couple, part tourist, part newlywed, discovering and sharing each other. They buy pots of herbs for the kitchen windowsill, and antique Staffordshire mugs for their afternoon tea. They visit art galleries and museums. They don't talk about the murder, though Phillippa reads an account of it, which her mother wrote while in prison, an account written in the third person and in impeccable style, not excusing the crime but explaining it as somehow rooted in a deprived past. Her literacy is such that one cannot accept this supposed deprivation. But Phillippa, now beginning to think of herself as Rose Ducton, accepts her mother as an equal. For the first time in her life she feels connected, however tenuously, to someone else.

Norman Scase, for his part, has been assiduously following every lead until he finally discovers the whereabouts of the two women. When he does, he makes detailed and elaborate plans to get into the apartment, stealing a key from the grocer downstairs, having it duplicated, entering the building when they are out in order to check the room layout. Finally he is ready, his knife sharpened, his final words rehearsed. He settles down to await an opportunity, a time when Phillippa is out, and Mary Ducton is left alone.

Norman Scase is a pathetic character, his frantic plans an hysterical attempt to wash away the guilt he has felt ever since his daughter's death. Why didn't he pick her up after her Girl Guide meeting? Why had he urged her to be a Girl Guide in the first place? So that her childhood might be a little less lonely than his, perhaps. He was ugly; even his own mother was repelled by him. Petty theft had given him stature with his schoolmates, until he'd discovered chess and became a master of it. With his marriage and his child, he had acquired, finally, some self-respect, but with Julie's death it all ended; his wife fell apart, accusing him silently, as if it had been his fault. Their marriage, or at least all that had been good in it, was at an end. Nothing remained to live for but revenge. They planned it together; they would kill Mary Ducton. And when, a year before, Mavis Scase had died, she made him promise to carry out the plan alone. He might have lost heart for it, but his dead wife would not let him. Not until their child's killer was dead, could he be free, both of his guilt, and of his wife. He had no choice.

The precipitating factor is the discovery, by Gabriel Lomas, of Phillippa and her mother at an art gallery. In his anger—at her seeming dismissal of him, at their sexual failure—he tips off a newspaper reporter, who begins to threaten exposure. Phillippa and Mary decide to escape to Brighton, but to do so they need money. Inexplicably, Phillippa decides to steal Maurice's silver spoon collection, instead of asking him for a loan, which he would certainly have given. When she arrives at the house, however, she finds that it isn't empty, as she'd expected. Rather, she walks in on Maurice and one of his students, in bed.

In the furious aftermath of this, she confesses that she'd come to steal, while he, in turn, tells her what he'd only hinted at before—that her parents had not given her for adoption because they'd been arrested for murder, but had, instead, relinquished custody much earlier than that, after they'd beaten and abused her. Quite simply, they hadn't wanted her. They had, in fact, fractured her skull, which is the reason she doesn't remember anything before she was eight.

Phillippa, enraged, hurt, confused, out of control of her feelings for the first time in her life, dashes back to her London flat where she confronts her mother as she had confronted Maurice and Hilda only a few months before. Then she had burst in and said, "Why didn't you tell me that my mother was a murderess?" Now it is that mother whom she wishes to hurt, and she cries, "Why don't you call me Rose? . . . I was Rose when you nearly killed me. I was Rose when you decided you didn't want me. I was Rose when you gave me away."

They fight, as only those who love can fight, precisely because they have loved, because they are hurt. They care too much and say things they don't really mean, angry things that arise from deep wounds. Each has been, in a way, betrayed, but Phillippa is the more injured, and it is she who cuts most deeply in return. As she storms out of the stage-set in which they have been playing out their carefully scripted roles for two months, she screams at her mother, "I don't want to see you ever again. I wish they'd hanged you nine years ago. I wish you were dead."

Norman Scase has been waiting for just this opportunity. The women have hardly been separated until now. He bides his time until he feels Mary Ducton has probably gone to bed. Then, keys at the ready, he makes his way into the building to carry out his plan of revenge.

Phillippa, of course, returns when she has run off her hysteria and come to terms with the realization that this turmoil she is experiencing is love. When she does, she finds Scase sitting, bewildered, next to the body of the woman he has attempted to kill. He didn't succeed, despite the fact that he drove a knife into her throat, for Mary Ducton was already dead when he entered the apartment, dead by her own hand, killed by her own conscience and her daughter's stinging words.

In this book's suspenseful will-he-or-won't-he plot, P.D. James has written a classic thriller. In the equally important story of Phillippa's unfolding feelings, she has entered the realm of serious fiction. But with the ending she has chosen, she gives the reader a conclusion that is pure P.D. James. The guilty are punished, the well-meaning are rewarded, and the whole is spun out far beyond its natural finish, so that all the various pieces may be put into place. She even has Phillippa, like Cordelia Gray in *An Unsuitable Job for a Woman*, cover up facts to achieve what she perceives to be true justice, lest someone who is essentially innocent be hurt further.

When Phillippa discovers Norman Scase sitting by her dead mother, she quickly decides to erase all traces of his involvement and to tell the police that she herself had plunged the knife into the woman's throat. She understands the anguish that has driven Scase to this almost-crime; no purpose would be served by making the facts public. He didn't kill her mother, after all.

"Won't you get into trouble? With the police, I mean."

"No. She killed herself. The knife wound was made after death. Doctors can prove that. You saw yourself that she didn't bleed. I don't think there is a criminal offense of mutilating the dead. Even if there is, I don't suppose they'll charge me. All anyone will want is to get the whole unsavory affair neatly tidied up. You see, no one cares about her. No one will mind that she's dead. She doesn't count as a human being. They think that she should have been killed nine years ago. She should have been hanged, that's what they'll all say."

So Mary Ducton, like almost all of P.D. James's murderers, is given the ultimate punishment, death. What the law could not accomplish, her own daughter and her own conscience do. Norman Scase, for all his elaborate planning, was never really necessary at all, and, with Phillippa's help, he is able to withdraw from the scene as if he had never been there.

Phillippa, predictably, turns for help to the person who for so long she has tried to deny, Maurice. And, as she knew he would, he takes charge, shelters her, sets things right again. She will go up to Cambridge as planned. Nothing has changed, but of course everything has changed, most of all Phillippa, who knows now that she has a heart—and that she owes this discovery to her murderess-mother.

The story, to this point, has been tense, taut, and exciting. The climax is just unexpected enough to cause surprise. It is disconcerting, therefore, to discover that it is not really over after all, and that the author has tacked on an epilogue. P.D. James does not like to leave her characters dangling.

Two years pass. Phillippa, who has returned to her original name of Ducton, is a student at Cambridge and a published author. She runs into Norman Scase one day, and he eagerly tells her the rest of his story.

With her mother's death, he had been able to shed at last the burden of guilt that had plagued him since Julie was killed. The score was even once again. He had begun to date a blind woman he'd met while tracking Mary Ducton, and they were to be married. Violet Tetley could not see the ugly exterior of this basically good man, and she loved him. He would be happy. The past is past and won't arise again to haunt them.

The girl tells him something of herself. Hilda, her adoptive mother, is happy, mothering a small dog. At last someone, even if only an animal, loves her as she is. Maurice is still teaching and lecturing. He took her to Italy after Mary Ducton's death. She doesn't tell Scase, however, that on that trip they had gone to bed together, father and daughter:

> . . . it wasn't, after all, important. What, she wondered, had it meant exactly, that gentle, tender, surprisingly uncomplicated coupling; an affirmation, a curiosity satisfied, a test successfully passed, an obstacle ceremoniously moved out of the way so that they could again take up their roles of father and daughter, the excitement of incest without

its legal prohibition, without any more guilt than they carried already? It had been necessary, inevitable, but it was no longer important.

It is a curious revelation. One wonders why it is there at all. What purpose does it serve? It isn't the first time James has toyed with incest in her plots. Maxim Howarth and Domenica Schofield, in *Death of an Expert Witness*, are very nearly incestuous. In fact, in every sense but the literal one, they are. But they are half-brother and sister, not parent and child.

The relationship between Maurice Palfrey and Phillippa is complex from the beginning. Maurice has a need to mold a personality, to play Pygmalion to a handpicked Galatea. It stems in part from his desire to be the adored, revered senior partner in a relationship, in part from his professional belief that environment, not heredity, is the determining factor in human behavior. It stems, too, from the fact that he has no child of his own.

He had suffered the death of his son, Orlando, twice: once, when the child died, at age three, with his mother in an accident; the second, when Maurice discovered, later, that someone else had been the boy's father.

He had tried once before to create his "ideal woman" when he married Hilda, whom he acknowledged to be his inferior both socially and intellectually. But Hilda resisted; she did not bend, she broke under his pressure. She failed him, he thought, though in truth he failed her, and couldn't acknowledge it.

Then he saw Phillippa—the child, Rose Ducton. She was oddly beautiful. She was intelligent. She was strong, unbowed by the twin burdens of abuse and neglect that had been her lot until that time. Surely this was a perfect candidate for his experiment. Surely, with her, he could create a woman worthy of his love.

So it was always there, this unspoken bond between them. They were more than father and daughter, though always less than lovers, until that day in Italy. But Maurice had left one element out of his equation in creating the woman Phillippa Palfrey: he hadn't taught her how to love. It was her mother, the murderess, the child-abuser, the convict-turned-Shakespearean scholar, who taught her that.

Phillippa was wrong when she said to herself, early in the book, "Who am I? Whoever I am, nothing of me comes from Maurice and Hilda . . ." On the contrary, nearly all of Phillippa does come from them—from Maurice, at any rate. Hilda had no role in their drama; she was faceless, a glorified servant. Maurice's tastes in art, music, literature, politics, even wine, are imparted one by one to the girl-woman Phillippa. She absorbs them, because she is made of the right raw material (Hilda was not), but they are his tastes nevertheless. They certainly are not the tastes of her biological parents. Phillippa owes a great deal of herself to Maurice Palfrey, and, somehow, in that bed in Ravenna, she repays it.

She is still, at the book's end, distant, cold, and basically unfeeling. She has learned the power of love—a power both constructive and destructive, she now knows—but the only person she acknowledges loving is dead. She wishes Norman Scase well, however, "If it is only through learning to love that we find identity, then he had found his. She hoped one day to find hers."

One is left with the very definite impression that she will.

Anyone who knows James's mysteries will find much that is familiar in *Innocent Blood*. There is the rich and detailed architectural description of which James is so fond (her paragraphs about the medieval city of York, where Phillippa goes to visit her mother in prison, are excellent) and her humorous put-down of lower-class taste in decoration, with its satin-ribboned curtains and artificial flowers, where tackiness fairly leaps off the page. There are, too, the many literary references, the quotes (attributed or not), the inevitable praise of Jane Austen, the device of describing a character by listing his books. There are knowledgeable comments on painting, on sculpture, on the museum world of London. All this is consistent with everything she has done before.

On several fronts she goes beyond her mysteries. Her use of symbol and imagery, for example, is extensive in *Innocent Blood*, far greater than what she has previously attempted. Roses are ubiquitous: Rose is Phillippa's name (which she rejects at the end, feeling it doesn't suit her); roses adorn tables in the adoption office, in the Palfreys' home, in Phillippa's apartment. It was in a rose garden that Phillippa and Maurice first met, and in a rose garden that Phillippa and Mary Ducton first encounter Norman Scase. Roses, when they are perfect, are lovingly described, their scent and sight intoxicating, but imperfect roses are made to seem a sham display, frowzy, overblown, messy, distasteful. Maurice, in his anger at Phillippa (for leaving home) and at Hilda (for not being Phillippa), suddenly decides he dislikes roses, because "flowers ought to be judged by how they grow. A rose garden always looked messy, spikey, recalcitrant . . . Why had he ever imagined that it gave him pleasure?"

Floral imagery is continued with the blind woman Norman Scase grows to love. She is quiet, timid, and shy, but she is also attractive, enduring, constant, and true. Her name is Violet.

There are other symbols, rites of cleansing and purification involving both water and fire. Several times in previous books James has used fire to denote the end of a relationship: when Adam Dalgleish burned Deborah Riscoe's last letter in *Unnatural Causes*; when he did the same with Mary Taylor's confession in *Shroud for a Nightingale*. In *Innocent Blood* she has Maurice Palfrey burn Mary Ducton's account of the rape and murder of Julie Scase, an account he has rightly guessed is nothing but a self-serving embroidery created for Phillippa's benefit. With that burning he assumes control again, though Phillippa will never again be the same as she was before. Still it is a symbolic ending to a relationship of which Maurice had disapproved.

Earlier there had been two rituals in which water was the purifier. When Mary Ducton and Phillippa first arrived at their London flat, they dropped Mary's suitcase containing the clothes she had worn in prison into a canal, and with that act flushed away the guilt and the memory of those years. Later, after their final fight, Philippa throws into the same canal the sweater her mother had knitted her.

> For a minute it lay on the surface of the water illumined by the lamplight, looking as frail and transparent as gossamer. The two sleeves were stretched out; it could have been a drowning child.

In a sense, it was. It was the child Phillippa once had been, the child she had only recently once again become. When the garment finally disappeared she "felt a physical sense of release." Running away, by itself, was not enough, but "drowning" the sweater broke the ties she'd formed and made her independent once again.

The characters in *Innocent Blood* are more complex than any James has previously drawn, but the book has one drawback on their account. They are uniformly distasteful. Even more so than in her mysteries, where people are necessarily unpleasant so as to be believable suspects in a murder, the characters in *Innocent Blood* are cruel, selfish, mean, and unhappy. That their reasons vary greatly is a tribute to James's inventiveness, but one can't help but wish she'd included someone, however peripheral, who could be remembered with pleasure instead of pain. Violet Tetley is the only one who comes close, but she is so shadowy as to seem almost unreal. Norman Scase is a would-be murderer. All the rest—Maurice, Hilda, Mary, Phillippa, Gabriel, seem bent on the destructive aspects of human relationships, pecking away at each other's self-respect, lying, cheating, belittling. Despite the somewhat hopeful tone of the final scene, one comes away from this book almost relieved to have finished with it. It is not a happy work in any way.

This, as much as anything, separates it from the mysteries. There is enough of the puzzle in each of them to make the reading of them a genuine pleasure for that reason alone. The same cannot be said for *Innocent Blood.* One cannot savor the unsavory.

5

LAW AND JUSTICE
Adam Dalgleish
Cordelia Gray

A mystery writer, if he or she is successful, can usually credit that success in large part to the policeman or private detective who appears from book to book and gives unity to the body of work. Peter Wimsey, Hercule Poirot, Miss Jane Marple, Roderick Alleyn, Inspector Grant—these and others like them have contributed greatly to the popularity of the "English school" of mystery fiction. And now, ranking among the best of them, must be added the name of P.D. James's sleuth, Adam Dalgleish. After twenty years and seven adventures, he is well known and, more important, well respected among fans of the genre.

ADAM DALGLEISH

In the nearly two decades since his introduction in *Cover Her Face*, Dalgleish has aged more than ten years; he has risen in rank several times, toyed with (and discarded) the thought of retirement, and published several volumes of poetry. He has become a little more of a confirmed loner than he was at the beginning—there seemed to be a chance, then, that he would eventually marry; now there seems none—but he has not, essentially, changed. He was substantially conceived in his very first appearance, and he hasn't been drastically modified by his creator in the years since.

He was described then, through the eyes of the other characters in *Cover Her Face* as "tall, dark and handsome" (Catherine Bowers), "supercilious looking" (Stephen Maxie), and "ruthless, unorthodox . . ." (Felix Hearne). To young Derek Pullen, under suspicion in Sally Jupp's death, he was "patient, uncensorious, and omnipotent, the father-confessor whom his conscience craved." To Sergeant Martin, his assistant in that case, he could "be pretty brutal." Mrs. Maxie thought he could be "all things to all men . . . a prerequisite of success as a detective."

In a sense she was right; to the degree that his job required it, Dalgleish could be hard or soft, demanding or patient, cruel or kind. But she was wrong in supposing Dalgleish himself was that changeable. He was not; he only appeared to change, according to the demands of the moment, and then only toward one goal: the solution of the case. He was then—and is today—absolutely single-minded in this regard. He has a job to do and he applies himself to it with an intensity and a dedication incomprehensible to lesser men. He lets nothing, least of all his own personality, get in the way of that mission.

He is one of those rare individuals who is able to see himself from a distance, to understand and analyze his own feelings as a dispassionate observer might, and to modify his behavior when necessary with an almost clinical detachment.

All this is made clear in *Cover Her Face*. When he first saw the body of Sally Jupp, for example: "He was never conscious of pity at moments like this and not even of anger, although that might come later and would have to be resisted."

Again, during his interrogation, there are several illustrations of this self-control. Questioning the maid Martha Bultitaft, "Dalgleish began to find this servility irritating but his voice did not change. He had never been known to lose his temper with a witness."

And upon meeting Catherine Bowers: "Dalgleish did not like her. He knew that he was prone to these personal antipathies and he had long ago learned both to conceal and evaluate them."

The Chief-Inspector, then, is a man of immense self-control. He appears, at times, almost robotlike in his dedication and seems to be unwilling—perhaps even unable—to give in to his own emotions. An explanation is hinted at when Mrs. Maxie, explaining her feelings about Sally Jupp's "engagement" to her son Stephen, says:

> "Of course I disapproved. . . . Would you wish for such a marriage for your son?"
> For one unbelievable second Dalgleish thought that she knew. It was a commonplace, almost banal argument which any mother faced with her circumstances might casually have used. She could not possibly have realized its force. He wondered what she would say if he replied, "I have no son. My own child and his mother died three hours after he was born. I have no son to marry anyone—suitable or unsuitable."

This personal tragedy, so far in the past, yet so much a part of Adam Dalgleish's present, is more fully developed in later books, but enough is explained here to make his aloneness understandable, and to explain the wall that he has built around his own feelings. Having been so devastated at a young age, Dalgleish was very wary of opening himself up to such pain again.

In his late thirties, Dalgleish has avoided "entanglements" with women ever since his wife's death. Yet he is still fairly young, with much of his life ahead of him. As *Cover Her Face* ends, he admits to himself that he is strongly attracted to Deborah Riscoe, and there is a hint that romance will develop between them.

Few of Dalgleish's personal tastes are revealed in this first book, but it is evident that he has interests and knowledge beyond what are ordinarily required for policemen. He appreciates fine art and comments on a painting to Felix Hearne: "Isn't that a Stubbs on the wall behind you?" To which Felix replies: "The cultured cop! I thought they were peculiar to detective novels!"

It is three years later when, in *A Mind to Murder*, Dalgleish appears again. He is older ("about 40, I should think"), and he is "on the brink of love" with Deborah. Still, part of him holds back. His wife and son have been dead thirteen years but "ever since . . . he had carefully insulated himself against pain." Marriage to Deborah—a definite possibility at this point—would threaten that protective wall he had so carefully built. His solitary life would be at an end, and he is very ambivalent in his feelings toward such a fate.

He has found an outlet for suppressed emotion, however. James reveals for the first time that her "cultured cop" is a poet, and a published poet at that. He is, as the book begins, attending a party at his publisher's, "which . . . coincided with the third reprint of his first book of verse."

> He didn't overestimate his talent or the success of his book. The poems, which reflected his detached ironic and fundamentally restless spirit, had happened to catch a public mood. He did not believe that more than half a dozen would live even in his own affections. Meanwhile he found himself awash on the shallows of an unfamiliar sea in which agents, royalties and reviews were agreeable hazards.

Dalgleish's thoughts of poetry and love are interrupted, however, when murder intervenes, and one gets the distinct impression that he is not sorry, that in his police work he is performing the real business of his life, and that all else is secondary, and not always welcome.

As it was in *Cover Her Face*, his approach to his job is single-minded. There is only one goal, and that is to track down the killer.

> She didn't know what she expected but certainly it wasn't this quiet, gentle, deep-voiced man. He hadn't bothered to commiserate with her on the shock of finding the body. He hadn't smiled at her. He hadn't been paternal or understanding. He gave the impression that he was interested only in finding out the truth as quickly as possible and that he expected everyone else to feel the same.

Finding out the truth as quickly as possible means he will use every psychological means at his command: ". . . he wasn't trying to irritate them or keep them in suspense [though] he wouldn't have hesitated to do either if it would have served his purpose."

Dalgleish has a particular dislike of delay, and almost compulsive need to "get on with the job." Felix Hearne noted this trait in *Cover Her Face*, and the Superintendent himself is aware of it in *A Mind to Murder*. Such impatience is typical of the kind of perfectionist personality that Dalgleish exhibits. So, too, is the attack of a migraine-type, stabbing pain behind his right eye, from which he suffers when he is extremely tired and things are not proceeding smoothly.

In later books, however, no mention is made of this malady. Surplus emotion is drained off into poetry, and Dalgleish has no further trouble with tension-produced migraine.

He becomes more and more committed to poetry, in fact, as he withdraws from other emotional involvements. A "second book of verse" is published just before his trip to Monksmere in *Unnatural Causes*, even while he is directing the investigation of the murder of a child:

> The child's parents had fastened on him like drowning swimmers gulping for reassurance and hope and he could still feel the almost physical load of their sorrow and guilt. . . . He had felt no personal involvement in their grief, and this detachment had, as always, been his strength. . . .

He may have maintained his detachment, but his next book of poems contained "the extraordinary one about a murdered child"— proof that he was feeling more than he appeared to, more, perhaps, than he wanted to.

Dalgleish's intense desire for privacy in his personal life has become, by the time he is in his early forties, as important a reason for him to avoid marriage as is his fear of hurt and loss. In *Unnatural Causes* he has to make a decision: to ask Deborah to marry him, or let her go completely. He suspects she is willing, therefore the question is up to him alone.

> It wasn't the loss of freedom that deterred him; the men who squealed most about that were usually free. Much more difficult to face was the loss of privacy. Even the loss of physical privacy was hard to accept.

He is torn. He longs for the warmth and stability of a good marriage, yet shrinks from the necessary sharing of himself that this requires. Finally Deborah makes the decision—she leaves, accepting a job in New York—but James has drawn Dalgleish well enough that the reader knows it is not only the right decision, it is the one he would have made himself.

He nearly didn't. At the finish of the exhausting adventure in *Unnatural Causes*, he longs for Deborah and pours his heart into a poem that he prepares to mail to her. Her letter comes before he has the chance. Yet how curiously right this all is, even to the fact that it is the poetry, and not Deborah herself, which is the receptacle of his feelings. This was, after all, Great Britain in the 1960s. Why didn't he telephone her when the desire for her overcame him? If he had, he might have reached her before her own decision was made, and their future might have been different. But he didn't—he couldn't; his emotions could not be shared directly but only through the medium of verse, and that fact cost him his chance to make Deborah his wife.

It is probably just as well. Being attracted to women, and particularly being in love, was very disturbing to him and not altogether pleasant. In fact, he likes women better without the distraction of sex. In *A Mind to Murder* James described his reaction to Frederica Saxon, a nurse at the Steen Clinic:

> There was no tension about her, no awkwardness. She had the directness of a schoolchild drinking coffee with a friend. He found her curiously peaceful to be with, perhaps because he did not find her physically attractive. . . . He liked her. It was difficult to believe that this was only their second meeting.

When, in *Unnatural Causes,* James tells the reader that Dalgleish's Aunt Jane "made no demands on him, not even the demands of affection, and because of this she was the only woman in the world with whom he was completely at peace," she is also declaring that, in the long run, he will never be content to settle down with Deborah, no matter how strong the attraction of the moment. He is a man who must have "peace" and "privacy," who must be in control of himself at all times, and the loss of control that comes from total physical and mental involvement with another would, in a short time, make him miserable. Under his surface confusion he knows this himself.

> . . . it came to him that he had got what he wanted at almost the precise moment of suspecting that he no longer wanted it. This experience is too common to cause an intelligent man lasting disappointment but it still has power to disconcert.

After the Deborah affair is finished in *Unnatural Causes,* Dalgleish never again comes close to marriage. He continues to be attracted to women—sometimes against his will—but he is careful to choose modern, liberated women with whom he can maintain relationships that are more physical than emotional.

Only with Cordelia Gray is there a hint of something else, an attraction that is based on something different from anything he has experienced before. Cordelia is, of course, only half his age when they meet, twenty-two against forty-five, so she appears to be something of a grown-up child, a perpetual innocent. Her naive (to his mind) idealism, her abstract notions of justice, only serve to make her even younger in his eyes. She is as open as he is closed, and, despite himself, he likes her for it.

Yet after a brief continuation of their acquaintance in *The Black Tower*, Cordelia disappears from sight, and she is nowhere in evidence during Dalgleish's seventh case, *Death of an Expert Witness*. He is more than ever the solitary, private man he has essentially been since Deborah left ("cold enough to be barely human," according to Detective Massingham).

> . . . how conveniently personal tragedy had excused him from further emotional involvement. His love affairs . . . had been detached, civilized, agreeable, undemanding. . . . His bereavement, his job, his poetry, all had been used to justify self-sufficiency. And the worst of it—or perhaps the best—was that he couldn't change now even if he wanted and that none of it mattered. It was absolutely of no importance.

James describes little, besides poetry and occasional women, of what her detective does for amusement. In *Cover Her Face* he had a thirty-foot sailboat, which he sailed in his off-hours, but it hasn't been mentioned since. Presumably he visits art galleries and museums; his knowledge of contemporary art is extensive and in nearly every book there is reference to it. His remark on the Stubbs painting in *Cover Her Face* has already been quoted; in other books there are these:

> "Who teaches you?" he asked. "Sugg?"
> "That's right." Nagle did not seem surprised. "Know his work?"
> "I have one of his early oils. A nude."   (*A Mind to Murder*)

> . . . there was only one picture but that was an original watercolor, a charming landscape by Robert Hills.   (*Shroud for a Nightingale*)

> the oil over the mantelpiece . . . looked very like a Stubbs and, thought Dalgleish, probably was.   (*Death of an Expert Witness*)

He likes "contrast in art, or in nature," the reader is told in *Unnatural Causes.* He likes contrast in music too.

> The pianist was playing Bach. Dalgleish paused for a moment to listen. Contrapuntal music was the only kind he truly enjoyed.
>
> (*A Mind to Murder*)

Music, however, is not a part of his life, as are poetry and art. One suspects that—except for such structured music as Bach—it is too emotional for him, too fluid, too free. He never spends time listening to records, except when he visits Aunt Jane, and he does it then primarily to please her. If he had a quiet evening to pass, he might choose to reread some of his "bedside Jane Austen"— who also happens to be the favorite author of Cordelia Gray and, not surprisingly, of P.D. James.

But despite all the fleshing-out of Dalgleish the "cultured cop," it is Dalgleish the investigator, Dalgleish the crime-solver, who is the focus of these stories.

He is not in any sense an eccentric, oddball detective. What he is is a professional policeman, holding, in his most recent adventure, the rank of Commander, schooled in traditional methods and relying more on dogged investigation than on sudden revelation.

"Never theorize in advance of your facts" is one of his maxims; it is enunciated in *Cover Her Face* and repeated thereafter, especially by Cordelia (via Bernie Pryde) in *An Unsuitable Job for a Woman.* Guesswork has no place in Dalgleish's scheme of things. Cold, hard facts are the components of his puzzle, and the more of them he can amass, the clearer the picture becomes.

Interrogation is one of his principal tools, as it is with any policeman, and when he enters a crime scene he usually isolates the possible suspects and interviews them one after the other, learning thereby each person's account of his own actions and a lot of gossip and hearsay besides. One of his favorite devices is to get people talking about each other. He has a particular fondness for cleaning women, servants, and other "background" people, who, as part of the scenery, so to speak, often know intimate details about others that no one else knows.

In the pursuit of facts Dalgleish will leave no stone unturned. He can be quietly gentle with a witness when his sixth sense tells him that is the way to be, but he can just as easily turn verbally brutal if such a course is demanded. He alters his behavior to the situation and may seem irresponsibly changeable to an outside observer. He is not. His every move, his every word is calculated to produce the desired effect. He is, as has been demonstrated, always in control of himself, and at no time does that hold true so much as when he is interrogating a suspect or witness.

Admittedly he has "hunches," which, among his co-workers, are legendary in their accuracy. But anyone who has followed Dalgleish through the seven James stories must know that he is not omnipotent. He does indeed follow false trails, and he does, too, have failures. His certainty that Nagle is the killer of Enid Bolam in *A Mind to Murder* is one example that springs immediately to mind; his inability to prove his case against Mary Taylor in *Shroud for a Nightingale* is another. He fails, also, in his attempt to get the truth out of Cordelia Gray (*An Unsuitable Job for a Woman*), and would not have been able—had she not left a taped confession for all to hear posthumously—to prove Sylvia Kedge's guilt in *Unnatural Causes*. He is classically successful in *Cover Her Face*, and cleverly so in *The Black Tower* and *Death of an Expert Witness*, but, interestingly, it is in these successful cases that he is most conscious of the pain he is inflicting on others during the course of his work.

Because he is introspective and a sensitive man despite his hard outer surface, he is acutely aware of his own failures in several areas. The inability to get the job done without hurt to others is a fact of his life he has learned to face, but it bothers him: "[the facts] were seldom discovered without some cost . . . and it wasn't usually he who paid." He would have brooded less about it if it had been.

He worries, too, about his failures in the investigation itself. After pinpointing the wrong suspect in *A Mind to Murder*, he remarks bitterly, "If this case doesn't cure me of conceit, nothing will." There is no doubt he remembers that and subsequent failures when, in *Death of an Expert Witness*, he states, "I'm bound to be [against capital punishment] until the day comes when we can be absolutely sure that we could never under any circumstances make a mistake."

There are many people, both in the police establishment and out of it, who would argue that a few "mistakes" would not be too high a price to pay for the positive results that the death penalty would bring, but Dalgleish is not one of them.

Among the unpleasant duties associated with the solving of a crime is the necessary "prying among the personal residue of a finished life," which usually falls to him. He is so much a private man that he is embarrassed for the person whose belongings he must search through.

Through it all, however, he maintains his detachment:

> He was too reticent himself to have any stomach for the emotional prying which gives to many people the comforting illusion that they care. He seldom did care. Human beings were perpetually interesting to him . . . but he didn't involve himself.

It comes full circle. Every discussion of Dalgleish begins and ends with the same conclusion: "He didn't involve himself." No one, nothing, penetrates his shell. He blames it on his job, but that is an excuse, not a reason. "His job, in which he could deceive himself that non-involvement was a duty," is the shield behind which he hides. Mary Taylor sees this better than anyone, and hurls it at him: "What would a man like you do without his job, this particular job? Vulnerable like the rest of us. You might even have to begin living and feeling like a human being . . ."

But then he wouldn't be Adam Dalgleish.

CORDELIA GRAY

By the mid 1970s P.D. James was ready for a change. Her first detective had proved immensely popular, but in *An Unsuitable Job for a Woman* she presents an entirely new image. Cordelia Gray is about as different from Adam Dalgleish as can be imagined.

She is young, only twenty-two; she is a private detective, where he is a professional policeman; she is essentially untrained, works alone, has no resources to support her work and no teams of specialists to call upon. She is small, almost defenseless except for her wits, and, of course, female. She is also the most engaging character P.D. James has ever created.

Cordelia has come to her present status in life really by accident. In fact most of her life has been unplanned, accidental, makeshift; she learned very early the advantages of adaptability. Left motherless at birth, she was brought up in foster homes for her first ten years. She wasn't abused, but neither was she loved. Her father, a self-styled "itinerant Marxist poet and amateur revolutionary," did not want the responsibility of a child and visited seldom.

"You must have had an interesting childhood."

Remembering the succession of foster mothers, the unexplained incomprehensible moves from house to house, the changes of school, the concerned faces of Local Authority Welfare Officers and school teachers desperately wondering what to do with her in the holidays, Cordelia replied as she always did to this assertion, gravely and without irony.

"Yes, it was very interesting."

Then at age ten she was, by mistake, ordered by the welfare authorities to attend a convent school. The error was discovered soon enough (Cordelia was, if anything, a lapsed Protestant), but it was never corrected, so Cordelia

had stayed on . . . for the six most settled and happy years of her life, insulated by order and ceremony from the mess and muddle of life outside. . . . For the first time she learned that she needn't conceal her intelligence, that cleverness which a succession of foster mothers had somehow seen as a threat.

There was talk, during this convent period, of A-Levels, and scholarships to Cambridge. Cordelia would have passed easily; she was a budding scholar, and the nuns recognized her as such. But it was not to be. "Daddy" suddenly appeared and declared he could, after all, use his daughter now that she was nearly adult. So ". . . at 16 Cordelia finished her formal education and began her wandering life as cook, nurse, messenger and general camp follower for Daddy and the comrades."

They were an easygoing lot, playing at a game of theoretical revolution, and they wandered from city to city, passing apparently unimportant messages around and accomplishing nothing. Their travels provided Cordelia with the kind of worldly education she had heretofore missed, gave her a sense of clanship for the first time, and taught her, most of all, a lot about self-reliance.

Then her father died, Cordelia was free, and she came to London and took a job as Girl Friday with Bernie Pryde's detective agency. Within a very short time, he had made her a partner, and then, discovering he had an incurable cancer, he killed himself and left her the business. Its assets were few. They consisted mostly of Cordelia's intelligence, her youth, her courage, and her perseverance. Money and reputation would have to come later.

That they will come eventually, there is little doubt, for Cordelia is as much a born winner as her late partner, Bernie, had been a born loser. She is, for P.D. James, a real departure: she is a totally positive person. Not only is she optimistic, capable, and clever, she is good-natured as well, at ease with others because, basically, she is at ease with herself. She may know defeat, but she will never know depression. Its seeds are just not within her.

This is not to say Cordelia is a Pollyanna. She fully acknowledges the rougher edges of life; she just is not chafed by them.

One of Cordelia's strongest assets is her clear head. She never panics, never reacts impulsively, always understands the ramifications of her words and actions before they occur. In this she isn't unlike Dalgleish. But she is very unlike him in that she does permit emotion—reasoned emotion—to determine her behavior, at least in part. Cordelia is not capable of total uninvolvement so characteristic of Dalgleish and, to a certain extent, of police in general.

Despite herself, despite Miss Markland's warning ("It's unwise to become too personally involved with another human being. When that human being is dead, it can be dangerous as well as unwise."), Cordelia finds herself becoming attached to the dead Mark Callendar. On the pretext of "getting to know the dead person"—a Dalgleish maxim—she moves into the cottage where he last lived, sorts through his things, wears his sweater, thumbs through his bedside copy of Blake. Growing ever more sure of the fact that he was a murder victim, not a suicide, she pursues her investigations not so much because she is employed to do so, but because she is inwardly driven. She is out to avenge Mark's death.

Cordelia is both innocent and worldly—a powerful combination. Her youth and freshness give her access to information, and to people who might be closed to an older, more typical detective, and who would certainly be hostile to a policeman. In this story, her only adventure so far, she fits easily into the Cambridge college-age crowd to which Mark had belonged and is able to establish a confidence based on age that Dalgleish, for example, could never have done. Thus she elicits confidences that eventually lead to more solid information.

But it is not only with her own age group that Cordelia has a rapport. Older people warm to her immediately, to her openness, her freshness, and vitality. She may be dealing in crime, but she bears none of the traces of that underworld of criminal behavior that beset so many other detectives. She is anything but hard-boiled. Only she realizes how tough she really is, under her coating of naivete.

From the time she first joined Bernie Pryde, she has heard of Adam Dalgleish. "The Super always said . . ." was Bernie's favorite way of beginning a sentence; Cordelia grew to hate the sound of his name even as she memorized (and began to employ) his maxims. Bernie idolized him, but she "had devised a private litany of disdain: supercilious, superior, sarcastic Super . . ."

When she learns, after her partner's death, that Dalgleish had actually dismissed him from his unit, she is all the more determined to dislike the cold, demanding man who had taken from poor Bernie Pryde the only thing he'd ever really wanted: his position on the Metropolitan C.I.D. Dalgleish's features, in her mind, become almost demonic. Yet she continues to apply his maxims in her own investigations, realizing, in spite of her personal antipathies, that he is indeed very good at his job and his methods must have a long record of success.

When the two finally meet they are at opposite ends of the ideological pole and can actually be considered adversaries. Cordelia has—thanks to her thorough investigation—discovered that Mark Callendar was murdered; that he was killed because he had learned that Miss Leaming, and not the late Mrs. Callendar was his biological mother; and that the murderer was none other than his own father, Sir Ronald Callendar, who was afraid that, if the facts of his son's birth were made public, the family's inheritance (used to finance Sir Ronald's scientific experiments) would be voided. When she presents these facts to Sir Ronald, he admits she is right but reminds her that she can't prove any of it—which is true. His confession is overheard by Miss Leaming, and she, Mark's devoted but unacknowledged mother, grabs Cordelia's pistol and shoots Sir Ronald through the head, killing him instantly.

This presents Cordelia with a knotty problem. If she tells the truth, there will be a trial of Miss Leaming, and all the details of Mark's murder (including the fact that his father had tried to portray him as a transvestite, to make the murder look like an accidental suicide-during-kinky-sex) would be made public. And to what end? Miss Leaming might receive a light sentence, or she might receive none. She was, after all, a distraught mother, acting on impulse. The Callendar name, however—Mark Callendar's name, too, although he was the victim—would be dragged through the newspapers, the subject of dinner-table gossip in a million homes.

This, Cordelia thinks, would not be justice, although it might be the letter of the law.

> She hadn't wanted him to die . . . but . . . she couldn't feel regret, nor could she be an instrument of retribution for his murderer. It was expedient, no more than that, that Miss Leaming shouldn't be punished. . . . Cordelia accepted once and for all the enormity and the justification of what she was . . . planning to do. She was never afterward to feel the slightest tinge of regret.

She and Miss Leaming fake a suicide, alter and conceal evidence, lie under oath, all in the name of justice. They succeed, and the matter is closed.

Or, rather, almost closed. Dalgleish hears of it, and surmises the truth, or at least the essence of it. It is for the purpose of getting Cordelia to talk that he summons her to his office. She is, however, a match for him.

She doesn't fear him, not in the physical sense, but she is acutely aware of the fact that he is a master at eliciting the truth from unwilling witnesses: "He sounded gentle and kind, which was cunning since she knew that he was dangerous and cruel. . ." She knows, though, that, if she keeps her wits, there is no way, this being twentieth-century England, that he can make her talk.

Their battle ends in a draw, when word comes from Italy that Miss Leaming had died in an auto crash, thus making moot the question of her guilt or innocence. When she hears the news, Cordelia does something disarmingly uncharacteristic of her: she bursts into tears. Dalgleish, relieved that it's over, reflects that he is "glad I shan't be encountering her again. I dislike being made to feel during a perfectly ordinary investigation that I'm corrupting the young."

They are so different, yet they are more alike than either will admit. If they could meet on a more relaxed level, they would discover that they both appreciate art, both quote literature, both like Jane Austen. Cordelia would find out that he is, indeed, "Adam Dalgleish the poet," whose work she admires. Somehow it must have happened, although P.D. James never tells the reader how, but in Dalgleish's next appearance (*The Black Tower*), Cordelia plays a minor role. She hears he is ill and in the hospital and sends him a bunch of wildflowers that she has picked and arranged.

It had been a small, carefully arranged, personally picked bouquet, as individual as Cordelia herself, a charming contrast to his other offerings of hothouse roses, over-large chrysanthemums shaggy as dustmops, forced spring flowers and artificial-looking gladioli, pink plastic flowers smelling of anaesthetic rigid on their fibrous stems. She must have been recently in a country garden; he wondered where. . . . It had been a touching, very young gesture, one he knew that an older or more sophisticated woman would never have made.

That is all. There is no romantic involvement, not even any hint of one, and Cordelia is absent altogether in *Death of an Expert Witness*. Yet she is almost certain to return in future James books, if for no other reason than because James herself thinks her "perfectly delightful" and has indicated a desire to write about her again.

6

MAJOR THEMES
Alienation
Death
The Cost of Crime
Retribution

Any writer who has completed eight novels has inevitably dealt with a number of themes. When seven of those books are mystery novels, however, there tends to be some repetition, caused primarily by the similar format of each book and the conventions necessary to the genre. Four themes that James has repeated in nearly all of her work are *alienation, death, the cost of crime,* and *retribution.*

ALIENATION

It is not surprising that many of James's stories deal with alienation. Almost by definition, a criminal, particularly a murderer, is alienated from society, if not in fact, then at least in his own mind, but in most of James's books, it is also true that those who are victims become so because of behavior that was the result of an alienated personality.

Sally Jupp, in *Cover Her Face,* kept herself apart from the world,

even to the extent of refusing to admit that her baby had a legal
father who might take responsibility for him. She could not allow
herself to confess that she was married, preferring the stigma of
unwed motherhood (and it was a stigma, in 1960) to the subor-
dination of identity that would result from taking another's name.
Had she not been killed, it is improbable that Sally would suddenly
have become a happy housewife upon her husband's return from
abroad. She seemed to enjoy her separateness too much; it had
been a part of her for too long.

Sally's alienation goes back to early childhood, when her parents
were killed and she was taken in, somewhat reluctantly, by an aunt
and uncle. Despite their vociferous protests to the contrary ("There
was never any difference made between Sally and Beryl. Never.
I'll say that to the day I die. I don't know why it had to happen to
us."), James makes it clear that the child was an unwelcome guest
in the Proctors' home. She withdrew into herself then and never
really came out. Lacking any real sense of belonging, Sally Jupp
found her fun in manipulating other people. "The real attraction
was seeing you sweat," said Deborah Riscoe to Mr. Proctor. "She
was only playing with you, pulling the strings for the fun of
watching you dance."

Sally Jupp was, of course, not a murderer; she was a victim, but,
by her manipulative and secretive behavior, the result of her
alienation, she enraged another person to the breaking point.

The student nurses who are victims of murder in *Shroud for a
Nightingale* are victims of alienation as well. Nurse Heather Pearce
is an orphan, a physically unattractive young woman, "dull,
conscientious . . . probably using nursing to compensate for the
lack of more orthodox satisfactions."

> There was usually one such in every nurse training school. It was
> difficult to reject them when they applied for training since they
> offered more than adequate educational qualifications and impeccable
> references. And they didn't on the whole make bad nurses. It was
> just that they seldom made the best.

Heather Pearce's failure to relate well to the other girls leads,
in her case, to jealousy of them and, finally, to a wish to hold
power over them. Since she can never do this by virtue of her own
popularity or even by intellectual achievement, she does it with

petty blackmail. She snoops and spies until she finds out something personal, private, threatening or humiliating about another girl, and then she asks a price for her silence. That price is sometimes money, but often not; at least once it is a promise to include her in double dates and other outings. Heather Pearce is trying to blackmail her way to popularity, but, finally, she blackmails her way to death.

Alienation has led Heather Pearce to search for power—to her, happiness—in unorthodox ways, and in the end she goes too far. When she is killed, no one mourns.

Jo Fallon, also a student nurse at Nightingale House, suffers from a different kind of alienation but meets the same fate. Fallon is thirty-one years old, in a school full of girls in their late teens. An orphan like Pearce, she is "remarkably self-sufficient . . ."

"She wasn't a woman to invite confidences," says Nurse Goodale, the last person to see Fallon alive. "When it was plain she wanted to be alone, I left." Whatever the cause of Fallon's disengagement from life—and it probably goes back to her parents' death in 1944 and her subsequent shuttling between boarding schools and rich, uncaring relatives—it is enough to make her an essentially isolated person who loves, and is loved by, no one. In the end it is her habit of carrying her whiskey and lemon nightcap up to bed every night, to drink alone and apart from the other students, that enables her killer to poison her so easily.

Illness as an alienating force is a major theme of James's work. It enters every book to some extent, but is best developed in two: *Unnatural Causes* and *The Black Tower.*

In *Unnatural Causes*, it is a physical handicap that causes Sylvia Kedge to feel separate from the rest of the world. Her legs are crippled from polio; she cannot walk properly and is disfigured besides. She seethes with rage against both the fate that dealt her such a blow and all those who, by remaining healthy and whole, do not have to cope with a similar problem.

Sylvia's alienation is total. Unlike Sally Jupp, who did love her baby son and may have loved her absent husband, Sylvia relates to no one in a positive way. She despises everyone, though for different reasons, and her considerable intelligence is employed for several years in her ingenious and superbly malicious plans for the murder of Maurice Seton.

James adds a special poignancy to this story, by making Sylvia's rage understandable, if not forgivable.

> Dalgleish was relieved to see her go. He had discovered that he did not like her and was the more ashamed of the emotion because he knew that its roots were unreasonable and ignoble. He found her physically repellent. Most of her neighbors used Sylvia Kedge to gratify, at small expense, an easy impulse to pity while ensuring that they got their money's worth. Like so many of the disabled she was at once patronized and exploited.

Sylvia is very aware of how people react to her. Few healthy people can comprehend what it must mean to be crippled or deformed or otherwise set apart from the general population by a physical defect, particularly a disfiguring one. Most do indeed feel "uncomfortably aware of their own good health" when faced with someone like Sylvia. The real miracle, James implies, is that most disabled people are able to subordinate their feelings of anger, even to eliminate them, and to live—despite their handicaps—genuinely useful and happy lives. The real miracle is that Sylvia Kedge is the exception, not the rule.

The Black Tower deals with Toynton Grange, a private home for the young disabled, which is, as the story progresses, the scene of a series of baffling deaths. The Grange's patients figure largely in the sequence of events, either as victims or suspects, and their characters, their hopes, their fears, and motivations, form an integral part of the book.

In *The Black Tower* James draws not one disabled person, but many, and she shows them not as participants in life (as Sylvia Kedge was, though to a limited degree) but as onlookers, withdrawn into the protective isolation of a hospital situation. Toynton Grange's patients are people who are unable to care for themselves. They are remote from life both psychologically and physically, and they react with anger, jealousy, deceit, and fantasy in their efforts to cope with forces beyond their control.

With considerable skill James makes these people come to life as distinct individuals, and though many are unsympathetic characters, she draws them so completely that the reader is able not only to understand what has made them so, but to feel their pain. Faced with a similar fate, she says, who would react differently?

How can the sick or disabled help but be alienated from a world that regards them as things instead of people?

Dalgleish recognized with transitory self-disgust that, however much he deplored Mrs. Hammitt's uninhibited expression, the sentiment wasn't far from his own thoughts. What, he wondered, must it be like to feel desire, love, lust even, and be imprisoned in an unresponsive body? Or worse, a body only too responsive to some of its urges, but uncoordinated, ugly, grotesque. To be sensitive to beauty, but live always with deformity. He thought he could begin to understand Victor Holroyd's bitterness.

Another aspect of the alienating power of illness is the fact that it forces people into accepting a subservient role, into accepting help when they'd prefer independence or favors when they would like to remain unencumbered by the gratitude that such favors necessitate.

"Well, no doubt [Henry Carwadine] is grateful to Mr. Anstey; they all are. But gratitude can be the very devil sometimes, particularly if you have to be grateful for services you'd rather be without."

Gratitude is a humiliating emotion, "no foundation for a satisfactory adult relationship, however transitory."

Worse even than the helpless loss of control that the sick or disabled must feel is their knowledge that, because of the barrier that separates them from the world, healthy people often do not interact normally with them. The ill are defined by their illness. It is the first and, often, the only thing that other people see when looking at them, and it arouses feelings of discomfort in the healthy, even when they are prepared for it: "All the patients were being helped to eat. Dalgliesh, despising his squeamishness, tried to shut his ears to the muted slobbering . . ."

Then, too, normal people often cannot stand the thought of the sick wanting to taste as much of life as they can. Anstey's sister Millicent says, with evident disgust, "Sex is for the healthy. I know that the disabled are supposed to have feelings like the rest of us but you'd think that they'd put that sort of thing behind them when they get to the wheelchair stage." It is no wonder that the ill are alienated, when they meet with attitudes like Millicent's. The "self-absorption of the sick; their preoccupation with symptoms and bodily functions" is not so hard to understand when one realizes that society almost demands such a reaction, since it contrives to deny them any other feelings.

This inability to conceive of the sick or disabled as total human beings with all the wants and needs common to mankind creates an unwelcome sense of guilt in those who are well. Massingham, Dalgleish's assistant in *Death of an Expert Witness*, felt, as he watched a terrified and neurotic Clifford Bradley, "the instinctive shame of the healthy in the presence of the diseased."

Dalgleish, too, knew guilt. In *The Black Tower*:

> He knew what Julius was saying. Here am I, young, rich, healthy. I know how to be happy. I could be happy, if only the world were really as I want it to be. If only other people wouldn't persist in being sick, deformed, in pain, helpless, defeated, deluded. Or if only I could be just that little bit more selfish so that I didn't care. If only . . .

The truly selfish don't feel any guilt; the great majority do, and are made uncomfortable by it. When the sick sense that guilt—as they are almost sure to do—they may react by using it as a weapon:

> He wished he could feel sorry for her but it was difficult not to watch with a kind of contempt, the way in which she made use of her disability. But then what other weapons had she?

The sick, the disabled, the imperfect all serve to remind the rest of the world of the tenuous thread by which their own health and good fortune hangs. Those who are life's victims may ask, "Why me?" But those who are spared have their own fearful cry: "Why *not* me?" The fact that there is no answer only makes the question the more painful to face.

Wilfred Anstey speaks for many when he says, "We all suffer from a progressive disease. We call it life." And we are all, James is saying, isolated and alienated by the disease of life to some degree. That isolation, if it is bad enough, may be even worse than death:

> "Mrs. Meakin, what you are doing is terribly risky. . . . Some day, a man will stop who wants more than an hour or so of your time, someone dangerous."
>
> "I know. . . . But at least I'm feeling something. It's better to be afraid than alone."
>
> Massingham said: "It's better to be alone than dead."
>
> She looked at him.

"You think so sir? But then you don't know anything about it, do you?"

Innocent Blood represents a departure from James's general treatment of alienation. It has its share of isolated individuals— Phillippa, Maurice, Hilda, Norman Scase, Mary Ducton—but, whereas in the mysteries the characters' alienation is presented as a root cause of murder, in *Innocent Blood* it is merely a starting place in their search for self. Not only Phillippa but all the major characters in this book seek to define their identities. Each in his own way comes to terms with his life, and each forms ties, however tenuous, that connect him to someone else. This is a definite shift in focus for James.

DEATH

Death itself is another of P.D. James's major concerns. The horror of a violent death, the sadness of a natural death, the maddening inevitability of one's own death, all figure in her works.

Every murder mystery, of course, deals with death, but in the "body in the library" school, it is merely an exercise in logic. James, however, feels strongly that death is not something to play games with. It is not something to laugh about, but an affront to humanity. "[Grace Willison] thought about Father Baddeley. It was difficult to accept. . . . Dead; an inert, neutral, unattractive word. Short, uncompromising, a lump of a word. Dead . . ."

Dr. Stephen Courtney-Briggs, in *Shroud for a Nightingale*, is perhaps James's best spokesman for this view:

"My dear woman, the girl's dead. Dead! What does it matter where we leave the body! She can't feel. She can't know. For God's sake don't start being sentimental about death. The indignity is that we die at all, not what happens to our bodies."

Death is seen not only as the ultimate indignity but as the ultimate separator of people. When a body is robbed of its life, it is robbed of all that makes it human and individual; it becomes not a person, but flesh.

Death, thought Dalgleish, obliterates family resemblance as it does personality; there is no affinity between the living and the dead. . . . There was no kinship [between the elder Lorrimer] and that rigid body on the laboratory floor. Death, in separating them forever, had robbed them even of their likeness.

96 P.D. James

Cordelia Gray, in *An Unsuitable Job for a Woman*, feels the same:

> Cordelia laid her hand gently on Bernie's hair. Death had as yet no power to diminish these cold and nerveless cells and the hair felt roughly and unpleasantly alive like that of an animal. Quickly she took her hand away and tentatively touched the side of his forehead. The skin was clammy and very cold. This was death; this was how Daddy had felt. As with him, the gesture of pity was meaningless and irrelevant.

But if death makes a person forever inaccessible to the living, it also puts that person on a special plane. If he was feared, he need be no longer; if he was loved, that love might now be acknowledged. Since the dead can no longer react, the living can be open and honest about their feelings for them, whatever they are.

> Thinking of her father and Bernie, Cordelia said, "Perhaps it's only when people are dead that we can safely show how much we cared for them. We know that it's too late then for them to do anything about it."

After the death of Sally Jupp, Deborah found herself thinking, "I ought to dislike her less now that she's dead, but I can't." Nor could most of the Maxie family, although Mrs. Maxie tried to observe the expected rituals because, "if people died in your house the least you could do was go to the funeral. Those who extended to others the hospitality of their homes should, if it unfortunately proved necessary, extend that hospitality to seeing them safely into their graves."

Rituals, however, are for the living, not the dead. And the living are apt to be offended by a death that comes at the wrong time. Dr. Epps, in *Cover Her Face*, "believed that there was wisdom in knowing when to die with the least inconvenience to others . . ."

Dalgleish, recovering from a serious (and first thought to be fatal) illness in *The Black Tower*, muses over the same subject. Death, he thought, was "the great unmentionable," and "to die when you had not yet become a nuisance and before your friends could raise the ritual chant of 'happy release' was in the worst of taste."

Good taste or bad, murder or not, the one fact of death about which all agree is that it is inevitable. Even if it is not perceived to be bad ("No more than birth is," says Inspector Blakelock in *Death of an Expert Witness.* "You couldn't have one without the other, or there'd be no room for us all."), it is still unavoidable. Dalgleish reads the memorial tablet to the first Wilfred Anstey on the Black Tower, coming to the final line,

> NECESSI MORI. Ah, there was still the rub. Death. One could ignore it, fear it, even welcome it, but never defeat it. . . . Death. The same yesterday, today and forever.

THE COST OF CRIME

Death is the terrible price paid by the victim in every murder mystery. But a major theme of P.D. James's work is not just this admitted tragedy, but the dreadful cost of crime to others as well—to the criminal, eventually, and also to all whose lives are touched by the deed in any way. Even the resultant police investigation is contaminating in its way.

If people who are sick or disabled remind us of our own fragile hold on life and are therefore unwelcome company, crime and its entourage remind us of society's tenuous social order and are equally distasteful. James sees police work as a necessary evil, but an evil nevertheless. "The police are basically doing a job that everyone wishes we didn't have to have done," she has said.

When the law, or its representatives, must intrude upon the lives of decent people because chance has put them in the way of a crime, they may cause disruption, suspicion, fear, deceit, and a spate of other unpleasant results. The all-intrusive aspect of a police investigation opens lives to a depth of scrutiny they would probably never experience otherwise, and many cannot stand such testing. Marriages may be strained, relationships broken, values redefined. Underlying problems rise to the surface and must be faced. Such an ordeal, even when brought to a successful conclusion, can seldom be looked back upon without pain.

In *Cover Her Face*, Mrs. Maxie's conviction in the death of Sally Jupp effectively ended her own life (she died within three years), and it ended the family's entire way of life as well. Stephen Maxie and Catherine Bowers, who would probably have entered into a boring but placid marriage and kept up the family traditions at Martingale, the Maxie estate, went their separate ways when Sally's death showed Stephen's basic selfishness so clearly. Deborah Riscoe and Felix Hearne broke up as well, and one suspects the reason had something to do with Deborah's attraction to Adam Dalgleish. Martingale fell into disuse and disrepair, as help could not be retained, and the village reacted toward the murder with thinly disguised hostility. Jimmy Jupp lost his mother, James Ritchie his wife. The Proctors were forced to admit the shallowness of their lives and their ultimate failure with Sally, and this removal of their crutch of complacency will have an adverse effect on the remainder of their lives. Ultimately the facts of the case will prevent any serious relationship between Adam and Deborah. He had, after all, proved her mother a killer. Yet he could not apologize: "He had never yet apologized for his job and wouldn't insult her by pretending to now." He wasn't sorry—he had a job to do, and he did it. If society was sorry that his job was necessary, that wasn't really his problem. In a sense, he is a victim, too.

The same type of upheaval occurs in all the books. An innocent victim in *A Mind to Murder* is Marion Bolam's mother, an invalid whose welfare was the motivating factor in Bolam's decision to kill her cousin Enid for money. "Mummy" will get the money, of course, but at what cost?—the knowledge that it was gained through evil, that her own daughter took another's life to get it. The elder Mrs. Bolam would surely, given the choice, have preferred her daughter's continued presence, albeit in poverty, to lonely, ill-gotten riches.

Jennifer Priddy, too, is a victim in this book. Worse even than the knowledge that her lover Nagle tried to kill her is the fact that she continued to love him and to hope for eventual reconciliation. Her refusal to face his amorality will cause her, one suspects, to ruin the rest of her life waiting for him. All the while she will blame the police who, she reasons, were the source of all her unhappiness: they forced his hand, by discovering his role in the blackmail scheme.

Nagle's crime—or, more specifically, its discovery—will probably finish his career as a painter, a career that was just beginning to win public recognition. Indeed, some in the artistic community feel that, because of his obvious promise, he should be spared from prison. Dalgleish muses

> "I wonder just how good an artist would have to be before one let him get away with a crime like Nagle's. Michelangelo? Velazquez? Rembrandt?"

"Oh well," said the A.C. easily, "if we had to ask ourselves that question we wouldn't be policemen."

Policemen, James believes, are not and ought not to be concerned with abstract notions of relative justice. "If they concern themselves with sociological theories, it deflects them from what they are there to do," she has said—and what they exist to do, clearly, is solve crimes. They amass the evidence, find the guilty party, and bring that person before the law, nothing else. It is not their job to worry about the side effects of necessary investigation, nor is it their duty to ponder the degree of guilt. That is why, in *An Unsuitable Job for a Woman*, Dalgleish is angry with Cordelia for her part in covering up the murder of Sir Ronald Callendar by Miss Leaming. He has deduced the truth—that Cordelia discovered Callendar had murdered his son Mark, and that, when Callendar almost laughingly admitted the crime, Miss Leaming picked up Cordelia's gun and shot him, and Cordelia knew: "She hadn't wanted him to die; wouldn't have been capable of pressing the trigger. But he was dead and she couldn't feel regret . . ."

The cover-up serves to insure what to Cordelia's mind is true justice. Callendar deserved his fate; a trial of Miss Leaming would serve only to hurt the dead Mark's name. Cordelia, because she is a private detective and not a professional policeman, may feel she can afford to weight the scales of justice and "play God," but Dalgleish cannot. Justice is, he tells her, "a very dangerous concept."

He is never so uncontrolled as Cordelia. He had felt temptation, in *Shroud for a Nightingale*, when he was certain of Mary Taylor's guilt. She, like Miss Leaming, killed a murderer. She was certainly not a danger to society and if permitted to continue in her work would do a great deal of good. Yet he knew her to be guilty, and he undertook the job of proving that guilt as a personal challenge, a vendetta. He is furious that she should even ask him to give up the search, or to omit from his report the fact that she, not Brumfett, was Irmgard Groble.

He said, "That's not possible. Your past is part of the evidence. I can't suppress evidence or omit relevant facts from my report because I don't choose to like them. If I once did that I should have to give up my job. Not just this particular case, my job. And for always."

The necessity to pursue an investigation to its end, no matter what the side effects, is nowhere better illustrated than in *Death of an Expert Witness*. There the Controller of the Forensic Science Service, Dr. Charles Freeborn, speaks to Dalgleish just before the latter sets out for Hoggatt's Lab, where Edwin Lorrimer has been murdered. The lab, said Freeborn, has "such a feeling of camaraderie."

Dalgleish said grimly, "I doubt whether that will survive an hour of my arrival."

"No. You chaps usually bring as much trouble with you as you solve. You can't help it. Murder is like that, a contaminating crime. Oh, you'll solve it, I know. You always do. But I'm wondering at what cost."

That cost, in the end, is terrible. James offers no ray of hope that Nell Kerrison will be all right. Her brother, too, will suffer. He will lose his adored father and no doubt be sent to live with his near-psychotic mother who, in Kerrison's words, "Made our life hell. . . ."

Nor is fate kind to Angela Foley, who has lost the only person she ever loved, the writer Stella Mawson. Angela will be alone once again, as she has been most of her life—a fate she has done nothing to deserve. If only Stella had trusted the police, and not gone out to meet the murderer on her own, she need never have died, but she—like so many people—thought police were nosy, prying individuals, unpleasant people doing an unpleasant job. And so she, too, was a victim and, through her, Angela.

Dalgleish does his job with all the compassion possible in a world where the end result is the only thing that matters. Unfortunately it isn't always enough. As he says in *Shroud for a Nightingale*: "I don't think it's possible to be a detective and remain always kind. But if you ever find that cruelty is becoming pleasurable in itself, then it's probably time to stop being a detective." James herself says in *Death of an Expert Witness*: "It was possible to do police work honestly; there was, indeed, no other safe way to do it. But it wasn't possible to do it without giving pain."

It is a point she illustrates clearly in every story she has told.

RETRIBUTION

Where Adam Dalgleish believes in adhering to the letter of the law, and Cordelia Gray in seeking her own brand of justice, P.D. James herself evidences a strong belief in retribution. The guilty must be punished. They must not profit from their crimes. Even when, by clever manipulation of the plot, she arranges for one of her characters to commit a "perfect crime" and escape the clutches of Dalgleish and the law, she adds the additional twist of fate that punishes the guilty party. In James's books crime never pays.

This is somewhat contrary to her claim of writing "real" mysteries, rather than puzzles; life is not always that neat. She admits as much but feels that murder is such a "dreadful, unspeakable crime" that she cannot, even on paper, help any murderer to go free.

An analysis of her stories will show that the guilty person always suffers imprisonment or death. Occasionally the final denouement must be told in a sort of coda, tacked on to the main story, and at least once it was carried over into another book.

This latter device was used with Mrs. Maxie of *Cover Her Face*. She was arrested and convicted of killing Sally Jupp, but the charge was only manslaughter, and her sentence was not harsh. Deborah could talk, at the end of that story, of "when Mummy comes home." Yet at the beginning of *A Mind to Murder*, James discloses that in the three years intervening, Mrs. Maxie has died. Her death was apparently a natural one, but Dalgleish feels himself "partly responsible" for it. Prison, obviously, has broken her health, and she did not long survive it.

Marion Bolam is about to be tried for murder at the conclusion of *A Mind to Murder*, and, though no more is said of her fate, it is clear, from the weight of the evidence, that she will receive the maximum sentence the law allows.

In her next book, however, James has fate, not the law, deal the final blow. That book is *Unnatural Causes*, and the principal murderer is the crippled secretary, Sylvia Kedge. With Digby Seton she has pulled off a very devious crime, and evidence will be hard to find. Digby, however, does not live long, for Sylvia kills him herself. That leaves only her to be dealt with. By law it will be difficult, by fate, however, easy: a storm of hurricane intensity sweeps over Monksmere, destroys Sylvia's house, and washes Sylvia herself off the roof to a watery death. Only a tape-recorded "confession" survives, to assure both that the truth be known and that Sylvia's name does not live on unscathed. The ego that had caused her to record her deeds on tape has assured, in the end, that she will be known and reviled as the criminal.

In *Shroud for a Nightingale* Sister Brumfett has, out of a misguided love for Mary Taylor, murdered two student nurses. She might have been captured eventually (Dalgleish was on her trail), but, before she is, Taylor herself kills her friend, after persuading her to write a confession that reads convincingly like a suicide note as well. Dalgleish, although he suspects the truth, is not able to prove that Brumfett's death was not self-inflicted. It appears for a while that Mary Taylor has outsmarted him. But Mary Taylor reckoned without P.D. James's retributatory arm. Feelings of remorse overwhelm her; in less than a year, she takes her own life—with the same poison she used on Brumfett. The score is even once again.

The Black Tower's final scenes have Julius Court, who killed several times to keep his drug ring from collapsing, die by falling off the cliff edge in a life-and-death struggle with Dalgleish. Again James has twisted the plot to provide proper punishment, for Court's involvement in the murders might have been difficult or impossible to prove.

Dr. Kerrison, in *Death of an Expert Witness*, confesses to his crimes in order to spare his daughter the ordeal of testifying at a trial. He will receive a long prison sentence, it is certain, the maximum the law permits in the absence of the outlawed death penalty. But in addition he has already begun to punish himself: "A murderer sets himself aside from the whole of humanity forever. It's a kind of death. I'm like a dying man now . . . I forfeited so many rights when I killed Stella Mawson . . ."

The most obvious of P.D. James's intrusions into the natural story line in order to achieve retribution is in *An Unsuitable Job for a Woman*. In this book, as has been discussed earlier, Cordelia Gray has covered up the murder of Sir Ronald Callendar by his longtime companion Miss Leaming, because she felt that to do so was in the interest of true justice. The cover-up works; the verdict is suicide, and Miss Leaming goes free—but not for long. Even as Cordelia is successfully resisting Adam Dalgleish's penetrating inquisition into the events of that night,

> There was a knock at the door. A uniformed constable came in and handed a note to Dalgleish. The room was very quiet while he read it. Cordelia made herself look at his face. It was grave and expressionless and he continued looking at the paper long after he must have assimilated its brief message.

. . . After a minute he said, "This concerns someone you know, Miss Gray. Elizabeth Leaming is dead. She was killed two days ago when the car she was driving went off the coast road south of Amalfi. This note is confirmation of identity."

It is all so convenient that even the reader who has been on Cordelia's side through the long confrontation with Dalgleish can't help but feel cheated. Mrs. Maxie's death was believable, Sylvia's was part of a complicated sequence of plot, Julius Court's the result of a struggle, even Mary Taylor's an outgrowth of her personality. But Miss Leaming's death is a bolt out of the blue— the fury of God, in the person of P.D. James.

It does, at any rate, have the effect of freeing Cordelia from further investigation. The Assistant Commissioner sums up the case with Adam:

". . . If I understand you aright, you suspect that Ronald Callendar killed his son. Ronald Callendar is dead. You suspect that Chris Lunn tried to murder Cordelia Gray. Lunn is dead. You suggest that Elizabeth Leaming killed Ronald Callendar. Elizabeth Leaming is dead."

"Yes, it's all conveniently tidy."

It is as tidy as all of James's work in this regard.

In *Innocent Blood*, retribution becomes one of the two principal themes of the book. Norman Scase has plotted for ten years to kill the woman who had murdered his little daughter. Revenge is the only thing that gives meaning to his own life; it consumes him, and, until he is able to satisfy himself that Mary Ducton is dead, he cannot be free of the guilt that has plagued him for so long.

The question of whether he will succeed or not gives the book its strong element of suspense. To anyone who is familiar with James's previous books, however, Mary Ducton's fate will never really be in doubt. She is a murderer. She must die.

Scase, during the course of the story, becomes a sympathetic character. His child has been brutally killed. His pain is vivid and real. Yet, if James permits him to carry out his plan of murder, she must insist that he lose his own life as well. Her solution—that Mary Ducton kill herself before Scase can get to her—frees Scase to enjoy a happy ending, the prospect of marriage to a young blind woman he met while stalking Mary and Phillippa.

In this symbol-filled book, the death of Mary Ducton becomes a ritual of cleansing for Norman Scase. He thinks her blood will purify him and enable him to begin life anew. In reality, it would not. Blood does not purify, in James's world; it contaminates. Luckily for Norman Scase, when he plunges the knife into Mary Ducton's throat, she does not bleed, for she is already dead. Her suicide has saved him from himself.

7

MAJOR CHARACTERS
Their
Social, Psychological,
and
Sexual Relationships

P.D. James's greatest strength is her ability to create characters. The people in her books are anything but paper figures; all but the most peripheral are three-dimensional, their backgrounds finely drawn, and their actions the inevitable result of the inter-action between their personalities and the circumstances that confront them.

The most prominent among them is, of course, Adam Dalgleish, who with Cordelia Gray has already been discussed at length. But beyond these two, who are the stars, there lies a huge cast of supporting players, a few of whom have appeared in more than one book, most of whom have not. Each is remarkable, with quirks and problems all his own, and there is little repetition of "types" from book to book. If they share a tendency to be unlikeable, that is more a function of the mystery format than it is of any basic pessimism on James's part. "Likeable people," James has said, "don't make good murder suspects."

The ability to create deep characterizations has been present in James from the beginning, but she has improved her art with each

succeeding book. She quickly overcame the tendency (present in
Cover Her Face) to paint some very old-fashioned, pre-World War
II British types, and has put forth more modern people in her
later works. The books seem more truly international because of
that fact.

Cover Her Face shows James's abilities just beginning to jell.
There are a few stock characters: Catherine Bowers springs to
mind, an essentially dull, plodding "nurturer" of the type popular
in romantic stories. She is in fact a nurse, and her ambition, it is
obvious, is to become a wife and mother. Equally unremarkable
are the doctor, the vicar, and Miss Liddell, the matron of St.
Mary's Refuge for Girls.

The Maxie family, however, is more diverse. There is the selfish
doctor-son, Stephen; his cool, intellectual sister Deborah, so attractive to Adam Dalgleish; and Mrs. Maxie herself, organized,
efficient, a loving mother, and a murderer. Yet, though the Maxies
have some depth, their backgrounds are not spelled out in detail,
and one wonders why they are as they are. It is their moneyed,
landed-gentry upbringing that has made them all so very self-
centered? Has their social position caused them to feel that their
needs and desires should take precedence over everyone else's?
James doesn't really make this clear.

She makes up for this weakness, though, with her portrait of
Sally Jupp. Sally, who is killed very early in the book, is at the
moment of her death only a black-and-white outline of a person,
but she is colored in—quite vividly—by those who knew her, in
interviews with Dalgleish after her death.

"Get to know the dead person" is one of Dalgleish's maxims,
and he follows it in this first adventure, as he does in subsequent
ones. This involves talking to the victim's acquaintances, her
relatives, her co-workers; it means searching her room, reading
letters or diaries, examining possessions. Of course what Dalgleish
finds out the reader finds out too; that is one of the "rules" of the
mystery genre, and James adheres to tradition in this respect.

Sally was a secretive girl, and not a very pleasant one:

> "She enjoyed the feeling of power that a secret gave her. Pullen has
> said, 'She liked things to be secret.' A woman I interviewed for whom
> Sally had worked said, 'She was a secretive little thing. She worked
> for me three years and I knew no more about her at the end of them

than when she first came.' . . . Her behavior wasn't reasonable. . . . It gave her the opportunity of hurting her uncle and aunt for whom she had no affection. . . . Not one of the dozens of people I have interviewed have described her as kind."

Although Sally was physically attractive, intelligent, and filled with the strength and health of youth, she did not find her life fulfilling. Unconvinced of her own worth—indeed, convinced of her lack of it—she could raise herself up in her own eyes only by dragging other people down. She was incapable of appreciating value in anyone else; her instinct was to belittle, never to praise. She sought satisfaction in manipulating other people like puppets, in watching them react according to which way, and how, she pulled the strings. Because of her physical attributes, because of her cleverness, because of an innate ability to put on an act if she sensed it was to her advantage to do so, she was able to pull those strings almost as often as she wished.

Sally trusted no one and confided in no one. She was sufficient unto herself, as she had had to be almost all her life. The only thing out of character is the fact of her marriage, which is revealed late in the book; yet even there, though she may have loved James Ritchie, she didn't trust him enough to tell him of her pregnancy. She let him go overseas for a long-term assignment and had the baby alone, passing herself off as unwed and laughing, to herself, at the do-gooders at the home for "wayward" girls.

Sally was so used to being solitary that she was unable to share, even with her baby's father, the truth of her pregnancy. To do so would have meant becoming less independent, and she could not risk it. What she risked instead—and lost—was her life.

James reveals all this, directly and indirectly, through the eyes of others after Sally's death, and the book becomes not just the story of a murder investigation, but a fascinating unraveling of a complex personality.

Cover Her Face appears to have taught James a lot about characterization, because her next book, *A Mind to Murder*, contains fewer stock characters and many believable ones. Marion Bolam, the murderer, is a disappointment—"the obvious suspect," says Dalgleish, and he is right—but many of the other characters are not.

Enid Bolam, the victim, is particularly well done. She is portrayed as a rigid, unbending woman with a stern sense of propriety, "one of those rare and fortunate people who never for one moment doubt that they know the difference between right and wrong." She is fair but basically unfeeling in dealings with her subordinates. She is humorless and censorious. Yet, at her apartment ("so neat, so obsessively tidy"), Dalgleish finds evidence of another life quite apart from that she lived at the well-ordered Steen Clinic. There, in photograph albums and other memorabilia, he can see her other self: a leader of Girl Guides, a patient instructor in their craft courses, a warm and friendly counselor at summer camp. There is correspondence with the girls and their families, letters of recommendation, advice on careers. She may have treated her co-workers at the Steen as objects; she may have thought of herself in that way, but these girls were obviously very important to her, their welfare very dear to her heart.

Peter Nagle is another of *A Mind to Murder*'s interesting people. Working as a porter in the clinic, he is a serious, and talented, painter, awaiting the recognition he is sure will come his way. During the course of the story, it does, and he learns that he has been awarded the Bollinger Prize for a year's study in Paris. Unfortunately, he can't take it up, because he will be in jail, for attempted murder, among other things.

Nagle is an example of someone who thinks so well of himself—albeit, as far as his talent goes, with good reason—that he thinks he can eliminate anyone who stands in the way of something he wants. The feelings and sensitivity that pervade his work do not spill over into the rest of his life; in fact, it seems that all his humanity is channeled into his art, and there is none left for living. People have no meaning to him except as means to an end. Jennifer Priddy is a handy sexual partner and a reliable model; in order to assure her continued presence in those roles, he pretends to be .in love with her, as she is with him. The fact that he will inevitably discard her when his need for her is finished does not occur to him as cruel. He simply doesn't think about it. She is of no more importance to him than his brushes or his paints. When, late in the book, he fears she may betray his role in the blackmail scheme, he doesn't hesitate to try to kill her.

To the end Nagle is unable either to feel guilt for anything he

has done, or even to admit that there was anything to feel guilty
about.

Even some very minor characters in *A Mind to Murder* take on
a life of their own. Colonel and Mrs. Fenton, who were among
Nagle's blackmail victims and were the first to blow the whistle on
the scheme, are memorable. Mrs. Fenton meets Dalgleish at her
home in the tiny village of Sprigg's Green, "gallant and a little
pathetic in the way she came down the path towards him . . .
looking up at him with anxious eyes which lightened, almost
imperceptibly, with relief." She inquires whether the Superintendent has come by car and to his affirmative reply she responds:

> "Oh . . . such an unpleasant way to travel. You could have come by
> train quite easily to Marden and I would have sent the trap for you.
> We haven't a car. We both dislike them very much. I'm sorry you had
> to sit in one all the way from London."
>
> "It was the fastest way," said Dalgleish, wondering if he should
> apologize for living in the 20th century.

Even truly peripheral characters have distinct identities. There
are, for example, the Worrikers, patients at the Steen Clinic
("Being precariously married was the Worrikers' main emotional
preoccupation"), or Ralfe Bostock, husband of Sonia Bostock of
the clinic staff ("He was given to malicious remarks, some of which
were clever, but . . . his wife lived in constant apprehension that
he would make the same witticism twice to the same people").
Almost everyone is introduced with some kind of descriptive
phrase that sets his or her identity firmly in the reader's mind.

This tradition is carried on in the subsequent books. The
principal characters are intriguing, the lesser perhaps odd, perhaps
funny, pathetic, or admirable, but never dull. *Unnatural Causes,*
which suffers from an implausible plot, succeeds despite this defect
because of its characters. Sylvia Kedge is the most original—a
strong, intelligent crippled girl who has reacted to her handicap
with an intense hatred for all who don't share it. The disgust she
imagines everyone to feel at the sight of her becomes a self-
fulfilling prophecy; people are indeed repelled by her, and she
hates them for it even as she is denying, to herself, that it is her
attitude and not her deformity which is the cause. Sylvia, whose

"great black eyes were skilled in inviting compassion" is malicious and evil, yet such is James's skill with character-building that one cannot help but feel some sympathy for her, mixed in with horror at her acts. She lives on in the reader's mind long after the book has been closed, precisely because she is many-layered, and her warped emotions become, at least in part, understandable.

But if Sylvia Kedge is unpleasantly haunting, some of her Monksmere neighbors are eccentrically memorable. Justin Bryce, "squatting on a stool before the fire like a malevolent turtle," had been, in his youth, striking, "but he was 50 now, and becoming a caricature." Elizabeth Marley, "heavy-featured, sulky and reluctant," had a passion for money, "rather engaging in this age when we're all so busy pretending to have minds above mere cash." And Celia Calthrop, a writer of romances whose face has a look of "spurious spirituality" "had dealt with love's counterfeit in nearly forty novels; but the coin itself had never come within her grasp."

Like her beloved Jane Austen, James manages to be both devastating and polite at the same time. The words she employs are as interesting as the people she creates with them.

In the character of Jane Dalgleish, Adam's aunt and only living relative, James has the opportunity to create someone who is neither a solver of crimes, nor a potential suspect. Thus Aunt Jane need display neither ruthless dedication to work, like Dalgleish and some of his assistants, nor that trace of madness or malevolence that immediately places other characters in the possible-murderer category. James says she is "a highly intelligent woman" who had spent the better part of her adult life performing routine parish duties for her father, a vicar, after her mother died, but had

> solaced herself with the study of birds. After her father's death the papers she published, records of meticulous observation, brought her some notice; and in time what the parish had patronizingly described as 'Miss Dalgleish's little hobby' made her one of the most respected of amateur ornithologists.

She is a fitting relation for Dalgleish. Like him, she is "obviously self-sufficient," matter-of-fact, and totally honest. "She made no demands on him, not even the demands of affection," which, however, "was there, and both of them knew it." She is given to long, contemplative walks on the beach, serious music on the phonograph, good wine and good conversation. She is tall, angular, strong, and healthy, and, because of her independence and her respect for his, she is "the only woman in the world with whom he was completely at peace."

Shroud for a Nightingale introduces another unusual character: Mary Taylor (the alias of Irmgard Groble), Matron of the John Carpendar Hospital in Heatheringfield on the Sussex/Hampshire border. She is a striking-looking woman:

> She was fortunate, he thought, to have been born in an age which could appreciate individuality of feature and form, owing everything to bone structure and nothing to the gentle nuances of femininity. A century ago she would have been called ugly, even grotesque. But today most men would think her interesting, and some might even describe her as beautiful. For Dalgleish she was one of the most beautiful women he had ever met.

She was also brilliant. She kept a telescope in her sitting room, to indulge an avocational interest in astronomy. She spoke several languages fluently. She quoted literature to Dalgleish (sensing automatically, it seemed, that he would understand her meaning— he did) and could converse easily about painting and other arts. She ran a tight ship at the John Carpendar, demanding and receiving excellence from her staff and displaying it in her own work. She was a model administrator, and exemplary nurse, a fascinating woman. She was also a war criminal and, at the end, a murderer.

The complexity of circumstances that could lead to such apparently contradictory behavior is described by James so well that Mary Taylor's character is made essentially believable.

Mary Taylor is at first very attractive to Dalgleish, and then, when he discerns her true role, she becomes the object of a near-vendetta on his part. She is guilty of a murder, and he knows it, but he cannot prove it, and she has declared she will never confess. He is never able to bring her to justice. Some months later she kills herself and leaves him a note confessing everything.

The suicide is the only melodramatic touch in an otherwise excellent story; it satisfies James's need to have all her criminals punished (if not by law, then by fate, or by their own hand), but it is basically unnecessary to the story and somehow out of character for Mary Taylor.

In *Shroud for a Nightingale*, for the first time, James makes the role of Dalgleish's assistant more than just a perfunctory one. Sergeant Charles Masterson, tall and broad-shouldered, and not unaware of his own good looks,

> with his strong face, sensual lips and hooded eyes looked remarkably like a well-known American film actor of the guts-and-guns school. Dalgleish occasionally suspected that the sergeant, aware, as he could hardly fail to be, of the resemblance, was helping it along by assuming a trace of an American accent.

Many of Dalgleish's subordinates stand in awe of the great detective, but not Masterson: "He had his weaknesses, but lack of confidence was not one of them."

Masterson isn't above bullying a witness if he thinks it will serve his purpose, nor is he a stickler for truth if a lie will loosen someone's tongue. He fancies the good things of life and generally manages to satisfy his large appetites even while on a case. He even sneaks in some sex with student nurse Julia Pardoe, a foolhardy act which, he knows, would mean dismissal if Dalgleish found out. But Masterson's versatility is fully tested in his encounter with Mrs. Dettinger, a witness who is portrayed as a blowzy, overpainted, worn-out habitué of garish dance halls, and who drags Masterson out to an evening of competitive dancing before she will consent to talk to him.

The detail with which Mrs. Dettinger is drawn is indicative of James's great care in this regard. The woman is an important witness, but not important to the story in her own right. She could have been a much simpler character, without affecting the course of the book. Yet James takes as much care with this kind of essentially peripheral character as she does with the principals, and of course the result is a richer, more memorable work.

By far the longest shadow in *An Unsuitable Job for a Woman* is cast by Cordelia Gray. However, there are several other portraits in that story that are worthy of note. One of the best, Mark Callendar, is not even living—it was his death that prompted Cordelia's investigation. He comes into focus, however, bit by bit as Cordelia delves into his past. Introspective, philosophical, literary, Mark Callendar was very different from his father, a man who seems to be playing the part of a scientific researcher as one would play a movie lead. A major difference between them is that Mark is essentially honest. That is why he was killed.

The Black Tower is similar to *Unnatural Causes* in one respect: its essentially unsatisfactory plot is overcome by its highly imaginative characters. In this book there is not one complex handicapped person but a whole string of them, the patients of a small nursing home. They are all incurably ill but suffering from diseases that will weaken—but not quickly kill—them. They therefore face the prospect of many years of progressive dependence on others, many years of a half-life lived in physical discomfort and mental agony. Each has compensated for this misfortune in a different way— fantasy, denial, anger, acceptance. None of them is happy. Some are at least potentially homicidal.

James describes them through the eyes of Ursula Holliss, herself a patient and shunted aside by a husband who was a little too eager to get rid of her:

> She had little in common with the other patients. Grace Willison, dull, middle-aged, pious. Eighteen-year-old George Allen with his boisterous vulgarity; it had been a relief when he became too ill to leave his bed. Henry Carwardine, remote, sarcastic, treating her as if she were a junior clerk. Jennie Pegram, forever fussing with her hair and smiling her stupid secret smile. And Victor Holroyd, the terrifying Victor, who had hated her as much as he hated everyone at Toynton Grange.

There is more to each of them, of course, than Ursula Holliss sees. There are many sides to each personality, and James, throughout the course of the book, allows the reader to glimpse many of them, either directly or by reflection through someone else's eyes. So Henry Carwardine is seen as a man of refined tastes, struggling to maintain his sense of dignity in an institutional setting, bribing an attendant to buy him wine and caviar and fine cheese, eating in the solitude of his room instead of the communal refectory. Victor Holroyd is a rebel, refusing to accept his infirmity, railing against misfortune, overcome with anger, and spreading hatred among patients and staff alike. Jennie Pegram, pathetically helpless and unattractive at an age when physical appearance is all-important, weaves fantasies to herself, tells lies to the others, and writes poison-pen letters to give herself a power she would otherwise not possess.

James knows that the sick, the disabled, and the handicapped are all too often characterized only by their illness, when in fact they are as diverse as any other group of randomly selected people. Because fate has limited the ways in which they can interact with society, however, their behavior may be extreme in one way or another. When they react badly to what has befallen them, they can become malicious (Sylvia Kedge, Victor Holroyd), devious (Jennie Pegram), short-tempered and sharp-tongued (Henry Carwardine), or pathetically hopeful (Ursula Holliss). They may use their weakness as a weapon, working on other people's feelings of compassion or guilt to their own advantage. The residents of Toynton Grange demonstrate all these traits to one degree or another; they are an unpalatable lot, but perversely interesting.

In *Death of an Expert Witness* Maxim Howarth and Domenica Schofield are brother and sister—half-brother and sister, actually, and they share a home and a cozy relationship that manages to exclude nearly everyone else. Incest simmers just below the surface of this boiling pot. It is never acknowledged, however, and Howarth buries his passion, while Domenica indulges hers with a series of lovers whom she uses and then tosses away like tissues. She is contemptuous of most men but not, of course, of her brother. He feels he needs no one but her and seethes with hatred at those she allows into her bed.

This isn't the first time James has drawn a close brother-sister pair. Stephen Maxie and Deborah Riscoe in *Cover Her Face* were another, as were Hugo and Sophia Tilling in *An Unsuitable Job for a Woman*. They were not so intimate, however, although in each case they were very possessive of one another, and prone to jokes and little remarks that excluded fiancées and lovers. Domenica and Howarth go farther, to the point where they have established their own relationship as primary, letting all others take second place. Domenica confesses to Maxim one day after Lorrimer's murder: "I can make relationships. The trouble is that I get bored and they don't last. . . . It's as well that we last, isn't it? You'll last for me until the day I die."

In the face of the bond that Maxim and Dom had forged together, any other relationships they made could not stand up. Each had married, but Maxim's wife had left him, saying she could not compete with his sister and was tired of trying, while Dom's husband, badly injured in an auto accident, dies accusing the pair of incest. Physically, they aren't guilty, but psychologically, they certainly are.

There are other uncommon relationships in *Death of an Expert Witness*. One outwardly happy one is that between Stella Mawson and Angela Foley, each of whom had met with failure in previous contacts but who found, in each other, the perfect partner. Angela is fairly young, basically insecure, a product of a series of foster homes where no one ever really wanted her.

> "It was like living in a second-rate boarding house where they don't want you and you know that you won't be able to pay the bill. Until I met you I felt like that all the time, not really at home in the world. I suppose my foster parents were kind. They meant to be. But I wasn't pretty, and I wasn't grateful. . . . Looking back, I can see that I wasn't much joy for them."

Angela, from her background of feeling unwanted, has developed an obsessive desire to please. She will do almost anything to be accepted, but, until she met Stella, she had experienced nothing but rejection, no matter how hard she tried.

Stella is a writer, older and more mature. Her marriage to Edwin Lorrimer had never been consummated, a failure that she attributed to him and that seemed to arouse in her a contempt for all men, as if he were somehow a symbol for his entire sex.

The two women met when Stella advertised for a typist and Angela applied for the job. When their relationship moved from the professional to the personal, Angela moved into Stella's small cottage; but despite a growing intimacy the younger woman never shed her basic role of employee. She was, in fact, a drudge, keeping the house, making the meals, cleaning up, dashing off to her nine-to-five job at Hoggatt's Lab, coming back home to lay the fire and then spend the evening typing Stella's manuscript. Stella accepts it all as her due. It never occurs to her that she is taking advantage of Angela, nor does it occur to Angela to resent her virtual servitude. She is loved and asks nothing else. Angela is a pathetic character the more so because Stella dies in the end, and she is left once again alone. She is bereft, adrift in life with neither compass nor anchor.

Another pathetic character is Nell Kerrison, whose cries of anguish ("like an animal in torment, yet so human, and so adult")

ring out from the pages of this book long after the story is ended.
In Detective Inspector the Honorable John Massingham, James
has created the most interesting sidekick for Dalgleish since
Masterson in *Shroud for a Nightingale.* Young, strong, courageous,
intelligent, he is the heir to a 500-year-old lineage that has—his
own merit, notwithstanding—produced "many generations of
amiable nonentities." Now for the first time there seemed to be a
chance for the family to achieve distinction, in the police service.
Dalgleish thinks him more like the son of a doctor, or a solicitor.
He is impressed with Massingham's work "and by his admirable
ability to keep his mouth shut and to sense when his chief wanted
to be alone." He is not unaware of the ruthlessness that lurks just
beneath the surface—a ruthlessness that is all too evident when he
deliberately goads Nell Kerrison into breaking her father's alibi.
Dalgleish hates him then, but he knows that it will all be
forgotten eventually. "He wasn't the man to destroy a subordinate's
career simply because he had outraged susceptibilities to which
he, Dalgleish, had no right." And he doesn't disagree with Massingham's response to Domenica's outburst:

"My God, yours is a filthy trade!"
"Not a trade, just a job. Are you saying that it's one you don't want
done?"

Dalgleish might have answered the same himself.
As she has in every book, James invests even minor characters
with peculiarities and nuances of personality not often evident in
mystery fiction. There is Mrs. Meakin, a "drab, sallow-faced woman
about 40" who plies her trade as prostitute near the little village
of Chevisham in East Anglia not from financial necessity—she has
a daytime job in a factory—but out of boredom and a stultifying
loneliness. Or Miss Willard, housekeeper to Dr. Kerrison, a
slovenly, foul-smelling lump of a woman who wears her incom-
petence like a signboard and oozes malice from every pore. Or
Mrs. Swaffield, the vicar's wife, "bringing into the room's cheer-
lessness a reassuring ambiance of homemade jam . . . and massed
women's choirs singing Blake's 'Jerusalem.' It was not, thought
Dalgleish, that she was unaware of the frayed and ragged edges
of life. She would merely iron them out with a firm hand and
neatly hem them down."

One of the best examples of a richly detailed minor character is Dr. Reginald Blain-Thompson. He

> had a curious habit, before beginning his examination, of mincing around the body, eyes fixed on it with wary intensity as if half afraid that the corpse might spring into life and seize him by the throat. He minced now, immaculate in his gray pinstriped suit, the inevitable rose in its silver holder looking as fresh in his lapel as if it were a June blossom, newly plucked. He was a tall, lean-faced, aristocratic-looking bachelor with a skin as freshly pink and soft looking as that of a girl. He was never known to put on protective clothing before examining a body, and he reminded Dalgleish of one of those television cooks who prepare a four course dinner in full evening dress for the pleasure of demonstrating the essential refinement of their craft. It was even rumored, unjustly, that Blain-Thompson performed his autopsies in a lounge suit.

Blain-Thompson appears on only two pages in the entire book, but, because of James's skill in describing him, he has more depth than many major characters, in lesser hands, might achieve.

P.D. James's characters, with few exceptions, come from the English middle class. She does not set her stories in the stately aristocratic homes of the wealthy, as, for example, Sayers and Christie often did; even less does she try to describe the seamy side of life. Her criminals are not hard-core, underworld types but ordinary people pushed to extraordinary means to solve what they perceive to be problems. Their crime is generally a one-time occurrence; it is usually true that even the murderers among them would not be likely to repeat. They have killed for a specific purpose, and once that aim is achieved, they would not be motivated to do any further harm.

In keeping with their middle-class status James's people are usually clean, civil, polite, and well-spoken. In circumstances other than murder they would be described as respectable. True, most of them are found to have some quirks of character that make them likely victims or perpetrators of crime—if they didn't, the books would come to a dead end rather quickly. But on the surface they are normal, everyday people, the kind most other normal, everyday people might know.

It is a curious fact of James's detective fiction that the victim is frequently portrayed in a worse light than the murderer. A surprising number of her killers, in fact, are not cold-blooded criminals.

Mrs. Maxie certainly is not; she killed Sally in a fit of anger, almost hysteria. Marion Bolam did plan her killing, but did so under pressure, in a frenzied attempt to secure some money for the care of her mother before cousin Enid could change her will. Brumfett killed two student nurses because they were a threat to her beloved Mary Taylor. Miss Leaming shot Sir Ronald Callendar when she learned that he had murdered his (and her) son. Dr. Kerrison struck out blindly at Lorrimer when the latter threatened to see that Kerrison lost custody of his children because of his affair with Domenica. Each of these people is desperate, pushed into a corner, forced to take immediate action—and they chose violence as their escape.

James does, however, portray the other face of murder as well. Sylvia Kedge, whose diabolical mind hatched a unique plan to get rid of Maurice Seton, commits a crime that is definitely first-degree. Digby Seton, her accomplice, likewise is cold-blooded, killing for financial gain. Mary Taylor eliminates Brumfett without apparent remorse (though that comes later), because she was getting in the way. Ronald Callendar kills his own son to protect his position as a popular scientist. And Julius Court performs not one but a whole series of killings, to keep his drug ring running smoothly. They are all amoral, their crimes free from compunction or guilt. Peter Nagle, whose attempt at murder (in *A Mind to Murder*) is foiled by the arrival of the police, is another of these amoral, calculating villains.

If, in creating distinctive communities with varied characters, P.D. James has made one major omission, it is in not including many contented, well-adjusted people in her stories. Nearly everyone has some kind of problem, some secret to keep, under a surface normality. Nearly everyone is in some way crippled, if not in fact, then metaphorically. These physical or psychological handicaps give rise to many peculiar relationships, which in turn direct the course of the story and provide a motivational basis for the action.

Not all these relationships are sexual, but many of them are. The almost-incestuous brother-sister bond in *Death of an Expert Witness* has already been discussed. There is another type of near-

incest in *Innocent Blood*, this time between a step-father and
-daughter, Maurice and Phillippa. This actually culminates in
sexual intercourse between the two, although, because they are
not blood relations, what has occurred is not technically incest.
The disclosure of their sexual relation still comes as a shocker,
though, because society's definition of the parent-child relationship
goes beyond the purely physical tie of blood. The coupling of
Phillippa and Maurice is very definitely incestuous, and, since it
is not really crucial to the plot (it is an addendum), one wonders
why James was so eager to include it.

Incest is not the only untraditional sexual attitude explored by
James. Lesbian and male homosexual relationships are common
in her work from *Cover Her Face* to *Innocent Blood*.

Many of the single women in James's stories seem to harbor
homosexual feelings, although such feelings are not always overt.
James's hospital-based books are filled with females who live
happily together without benefit of male companionship. Sister
Ambrose, in a *A Mind to Murder*,

> lived with an elderly nurse friend . . . together they had bought a
> house . . . and lived together for 20 years on their joint income in
> comfort and happy accord. Neither of them had married and neither
> of them regretted it.

Sister Brumfett, in *Shroud for a Nightingale*, is attached to Matron
Mary Taylor like a puppy to its master. Her adoring, subservient
love is probably not returned, Dalgleish thinks: "When, and with
whom, did she find her consolation? In her job? . . . In astronomy?
. . . With Brumfett? Surely to God not with Brumfett!"

His repulsion at the thought of a Brumfett-Taylor alliance is
based, however, not so much on the fact that they are both women
as on the fact that Brumfett was in no way Taylor's intellectual
equal. That, and that alone, would have made true intimacy
between them unthinkable, in Dalgleish's eyes.

Sister Rolfe, in the same book, is conducting a one-sided affair
with student nurse Julia Pardoe. Pardoe is just using the older
woman for her own ends—she's quite obviously heterosexual and
has a fleeting encounter with Dalgleish's assistant Masterson later
in the story—and Rolfe is made to seem rather pathetic, as she
tries to hold on to Julia after the girl has begun to break away.

Perfectly contented in their relationship are Miss Beale and Miss Burrows, whose shared life and mutual admiration are described in the beginning of the book as Miss Beale makes preparations for a visit to the John Carpendar Hospital: "the happiest marriages are sustained by such illusions and [their] very different . . . relationship was similarly founded."

A lesbian relationship is very clearly indicated in *Death of an Expert Witness* in the household shared by Angela Foley and Stella Mawson. Angela speaks of Stella lovingly after learning of her death,

> "Star was so small and fragile, and her heart wasn't strong. When I put my arms around her it was like holding a bird. . . . I shall never see her again. . . . I don't believe it yet. I know that it must be true or you wouldn't be here, but I still don't believe it. How shall I bear it when I do?"

Again in *Innocent Blood* the issue of lesbianism is raised when Phillippa visits her mother in prison and says,

> "You mean they're lovers, lesbians? Is there a lot of that in prison?"
> Her mother smiled.
> "You make it sound like an infectious disease. Of course it happens. It happens often. People need to be loved. They need to feel that they matter to someone . . ."

James's treatment of this subject ranges from tacit acceptance, in the early books, to the near-complete approval evidenced in the last two examples. At no time is she cruel or cutting in her remarks about lesbians. The same cannot be said, however, for her characterizations of male homosexuals, which are frequently derisive.

In *Unnatural Causes* Digby Seton, half-brother of the murdered man, is described by Elizabeth Marley as a "pansy." And Digby says of himself, "He was afraid, too, that I might set up house with a queer. He didn't want his money shared with a pansy boyfriend. Poor old Maurice!"

Justin Bryce, another of the Monksmere residents who is a possible suspect in the crime, is described as having delicate hands, soft skin, a fussy disposition, and a passion for cats. Lest anyone still be in the dark regarding his sexual orientation, James has him say, "[at the theater] I was with Paul Markham, such a sensitive boy. He was in tears by the end of the first act."

And in discussing the murder, Inspector Reckless says to Dalgleish, "They're a spiteful lot, queers. Not violent on the whole. But spiteful. And there was a spiteful crime . . ."

Sexual deviation is mentioned only briefly in *An Unsuitable Job for a Woman*, when it is discovered that Mark Callendar had been dressed in women's underwear and made up with rouge and lipstick by his killer, who was trying to make the death look like the accidental result of some unconventional sexual experimentation. Mark, however, hadn't really been a homosexual or a transvestite, and the ploy didn't work.

The Black Tower presents several different homosexual relationships. Julius Court has had a minor affair with Dennis Lerner, a male nurse, during the course of the story, and at the end he explains to Dalgleish why he'd carried on the trade in illicit drugs:

> "I could take you to pubs in Westminster—Christ, you probably know them—and bring you face to face with what I fear; the pathetic elderly queens managing on their pensions. . . . I'm not ashamed of my nature. But if I'm to live at all, I have to be rich . . ."

Court is presented as the usual effeminate caricature and is described by Dalgleish himself as "a hysterical queer." But Henry Carwadine is drawn more sympathetically. And, when the story is told of how he began to share a mutual love with seventeen-year-old Peter Bonnington, it comes as a surprise because the author has not painted him as a stereotypical homosexual. He is simply a man in need of love.

In *Innocent Blood* it is Gabriel Lomas who is, if not truly homosexual, at least bisexual. Phillippa treats him with contempt at the conclusion of their brief sexual encounter: "Why did you bother? Was it to prove you can make it with a woman?"

He had answered with an equally nasty retort and had nursed his wound for months until the opportunity for revenge presented itself—proving once again, in Reckless's words, that "they're a spiteful lot, queers."

Still other relationships are dissected in James's work. Parents and children have a host of difficulties, the results of which turn up, in many cases, decades later. Childhood abuse, abandonment, and manipulation are the causes of much of the personality disturbance she relates and eventually lead, at least in some instances, to murder.

Innocent Blood is perhaps the most striking example of this mistreatment of children. Mary Ducton's father beat her for pleasure, it is disclosed. Norman Scase was ridiculed by his own mother because of his ugly face. Phillippa was abused by the Ductons, and later treated as an object by Maurice. Maurice himself is traumatized by the discovery that the dead Orlando was actually fathered by another man.

Because of the tumultuous nature of the various parent-child relationships in this book, all other relationships are muddled, as the different characters struggle to come to terms with their misplaced identities. Both love and hate are expressed in unconventional ways, from Maurice's incestuous desire for Phillippa to Mary Ducton's killing of the child Julie Scase, because "she couldn't bear to hear a child crying." That early childhood experiences are important molders of later life is an obvious conclusion to draw from *Innocent Blood*, as it is from earlier James works.

A number of James's characters are orphans, their lonely upbringing often contributing heavily to their later fate. Sally Jupp, whose remoteness cost her her life, was brought up by an uncaring aunt and uncle. She never felt she belonged to anyone. Angela Foley was so misshapen by life in a series of foster homes that she could find happiness only in near-servitude to another, older woman. Was Stella Mawson a stand-in for the mother Angela never had?

Heather Pearce and Jo Fallon, victims of murder in *Shroud for a Nightingale*, were both orphans, whose lack of a warm family life contributed to their inability, as adults, to relate normally to others. That inability, in turn, played a part in the subsequent turn of events.

Enid Bolam, who never married, nevertheless loved children and ran a Girl Guide troop. That her maternal feelings toward the young girls might have been mingled with less acceptable sexual feelings is never stated, but the possibility is implied. Phillippa's father, Martin Ducton, also had an uncommon interest in children, but unlike Enid Bolam he could not suppress it. It led, of course, to the rape and murder of Julie Scase.

Marital relationships, like the other relationships discussed here, are frequently stormy. Almost the only happy marriages in James's work are those of the dull, placid, working classes. The educated middle class—that is, most of the main characters—do not get along so well. Husbands cheat on wives, wives snipe at husbands, partners are bored with each other sexually and intellectually, and in general the only contented people are those who are single.

It is interesting to note that James, although long a successful blender of the dual roles of wife and career woman, does not portray any women in her books who happily combine these two functions. In much of her work, in fact, she consistently reinforces old-fashioned images that tended to classify women and keep them "in their place." Her main character, Adam Dalgleish, embodies many chauvinistic attitudes.

Thinking about Frederica Saxon, a nurse at the Steen Clinic, Dalgleish feels that, although "he liked her . . . there was something about her certainty, her self-sufficiency, which he found irritating." Like many men of his age, he feels threatened by a self-sufficient woman and reacts with dislike. Women are supposed to be dependent, according to his creed. Marriage is their only real goal:

> "This ambition [of Enid Bolam's] for Miss Priddy's future career struck Dalgleish as a little odd. The child gave no impression of being ambitious and she would surely marry in time."

That she might want to work after that marriage would be unthinkable. Women worked, or they were housewives; they didn't do both, and they didn't choose the former course if they had an option.

Dalgleish, in his comments and asides, reveals other stereotypical attitudes as well. Speaking of Marion Bolam in *A Mind to Murder* he says, "she feels no particular guilt, I suspect, except the usual female guilt at being found out." Even in the late 1970s, in *The Black Tower*, Dalgleish retains his old attitudes:

> His love affairs . . . had been detached, civilized, agreeable, undemanding. It was understood that his time was never completely his own but that his heart most certainly was. The women were liberated. They had interesting jobs, agreeable flats, they were adept at settling for what they could get. Certainly they were liberated from the messy, clogging, disruptive emotions which embroiled other female lives . . .

He wonders what his "carefully-spaced encounters" could possibly have to do with love. The reader may wonder, in turn, how he could even hope to feel real love for a member of a sex he puts down so decisively. One can feel a sort of protective affection for the "little woman," but a true love between equals is impossible if one of the partners believes, even subconsciously, that he is intrinsically superior by reason of his sex.

It seems unlikely that Dalgleish would make the statements he makes about women if the author did not share his views. Indeed, she puts similar deprecating remarks in the mouths of other characters as well. In *Cover Her Face*, Deborah says of Felix, "He had a woman's interest in the small change of life . . . ," and in the same book James says that Mr. Bocock, "although he lived alone . . . had the woman's habit of putting everything edible on the table at once . . ." It is a gratuitous remark, and one wonders why it had to be made at all.

Cover Her Face is filled with such comments. They reflect a pre-1960s attitude in many ways, especially with regard to sexual customs. An example is the talk of "wayward" girls at the home for unwed mothers. In writing "Sally was an excellent little worker and a most deserving girl who was doing her best to atone for her mistake" (i.e., having a baby), James is keeping to the tone and traditional viewpoint of an earlier time.

The basic goal of women in *Cover Her Face* is to find a husband and raise a family. Sally plays the game, even though she is secretly married. Deborah, who hates Sally "because she has a child and I haven't," toys with the idea of marrying Felix, although she doesn't love him, and finds herself disconcerted when the expected offer does not materialize. Catherine Bowers is determined to marry Stephen, but, when that falls through, she settles happily for James Ritchie.

There is not quite so much emphasis on husband-hunting in James's next book, *A Mind to Murder*, but there are still some surprising remarks, surprising, when one considers that they were written by a woman who was herself a hospital administrator, which is not a "female" position. Nagle, describing Mrs. Bostock, says she will undoubtedly scheme to get the dead Enid Bolam's job: "You couldn't miss compulsive ambition in a woman. They burnt with it. You could almost smell it sizzling their flesh."

The curious reader is left to wonder how James would have had Nagle describe compulsive ambition in a man.

Another surprising remark in *A Mind to Murder* concerns a physician, Dr. Albertine Maddox. A surgeon, she has also qualified as a psychiatrist and is certainly a successful woman by any standard. Why, then, did James say she ". . . looked like what she was, the comfortable mother of a family . . ." And worse, after creating a woman who is the antithesis of "just a housewife" she goes on: "She had five children, the sons intelligent and prosperous, the girls well-married." It is an incomprehensible remark, out of place and out of date even in the early 1960s.

An Unsuitable Job for a Woman, although it introduces a gutsy heroine, Cordelia Gray, still contains some trace of the old prejudice. Talking about the dead Mrs. Callendar, Elizabeth Leaming remarks, ". . . she hadn't been much success as a woman [because she couldn't bear a child]. If she lost her husband, what else was there for her?"

Shroud for a Nightingale, set as it is in a nearly all-female situation, abounds with old-fashioned fussy old maids and silly young girls who seem dated for a book written in the early 1970s. Several of the student nurses are discussed in the following manner:

(Diane Harper)
"We all thought it was silly of her to give up so near to her finals but her father has never been keen on her training as a nurse and she is engaged to be married anyway, so I suppose she thought it didn't matter."

(Nurse Goodale)
". . . one of our most efficient nurses. I was hoping that she would stay on after her training to take a post as a staff nurse. But that is hardly likely. She's engaged to our local vicar and they want to marry next Easter. . . . Another good career lost to the profession, but she knows her own priorities I suppose."

It's almost a period piece instead of a modern novel. The assumption that a girl would abandon her nursing career immediately upon marriage seems especially strange coming from James, who had long been a working wife and mother. Somehow it doesn't ring true, even for its time; it is almost laughably quaint today.

Even in *Death of an Expert Witness* James includes a few antifemale passages. Maxim Howarth, speaking to Edwin Lorrimer, sneers,

"The fact that you can't take criticism without becoming as personal and spiteful as a neurotic girl is an example of what I mean." Describing Claire Easterbrook, Senior Biologist at Hoggatt's Lab, James says, "She was a thin, long-waisted girl of about thirty . . ." Feminists would blanch at the word "girl" used for a woman of thirty. It is surely unintentional, and simply illustrates the fact that many people—particularly those who are no longer young—have internalized certain "sexist" words and don't even realize they are using them. Ironically James makes a point of the fact that Easterbrook insists on being called Ms. It's the first time James has used this term, but, teamed with the word "girl," it shows that the author has a long way to go before she has fully modernized her language.

Even in this book, written in 1977, young women are still struggling with the (apparent) problem of marriage vs. career. Young Brenda Pridmore works at Hoggatt's as receptionist and is fascinated by the work of the lab. Lorrimer takes an interest in her and encourages her to study science with an eye toward a more responsible job there in the future. She's bright, eager, enthusiastic; she seems a perfect candidate. But Gerald Bowlem is waiting in the wings:

"Mum and Dad . . . want me to marry Gerald Bowlem. I think I would like to marry Gerald, at least, I've never thought of marrying anyone else, but not just yet. It would be nice to be a scientist and have a proper career first . . ."

It is strange that even in the late 1970s James seems to think young women are making the same either-or choices they did a generation before.

The other side of the female-stereotype coin is the fact that women, too, are guilty of the same tunnel vision they decry in men. P.D. James's women illustrate this in several books:

"Being a man, he was flattered to be asked for advice."

(A Mind to Murder)

"You should have had more pride than to let him use you as a household drudge. Men prefer a little spirit, you know."

(Unnatural Causes)

"What is there to be frightened of? We shall be dealing only with men."

(An Unsuitable Job for a Woman)

Obviously, P.D. James does not fully believe in all the foregoing statements—about either men or women. Her own life and career stand in direct opposition to many of them. But it is clear that, despite her own successes, she is not herself a feminist in the activist sense of the word.

Many women of her generation who had "made it" on their own consider themselves different from (and superior to) the majority of their own sex. Instead of rejecting the notion that women are frivolous, emotional, irrational, etc., such women agree that the stereotypes are valid—but not for them. Basically they don't like other women very much, preferring the company of men and, if asked, will assert that they have achieved their success by assuming positive "masculine" traits and rejecting the negative "feminine" ones. They tend almost to apologize for their sex, which feminists do not.

There is no direct evidence that P.D. James fits into this group, but her use of initials in her pen name strongly suggests a desire not to be labeled as a woman. Such camouflage may have been necessary at one time in history, but it certainly was not when her career began, for such women as Christie, Sayers, Allingham, Marsh, and Tey had demonstrated that women not only could write excellent murder mysteries but could win tremendous popular acclaim as well. If anything, a female name was an asset, not a liability, in the English mystery field. Yet James chose not to be known as a woman in her first efforts, though she never attempted to deny her identity—only to obscure it. She wanted to be judged by results, not by her sex. It was, however, not long before her full name was common knowledge and the use of initials was, in effect, a short-lived statement rather than a permanent shield.

James's women generally fall into four groups: "liberated" career women, always cold and aggressively unattached; homebodies, dull and vapid; silly young girls searching for a man; old maids who work because they have no choice and who—often by preference, though sometimes not—live in a female world. There is a real dearth of modern, intelligent working women who are married or otherwise involved in a stable long-term relationship with a man. She insists that this omission does not mean that she believes such people do not exist. It is rather, she says, that they do not make very good subjects for a mystery novel. Still, it is curious that she has not included a few, if only on the periphery of her stories.

In her selection of villains and victims, James is even-handed, choosing men and women with almost equal frequency. Neither sex has a monopoly on good or evil; if anything, the most hideous crimes are perpetrated by women. What can be more diabolical than Sylvia Kedge's scheme to frighten Maurice Seton to death by sealing him into a coffin, thus making his recurrent nightmare of claustrophobia come true? What can be more cruel than Brumfett's murder of Heather Pearce by carbolic acid in the intragastric feed? Compared to these methods, a strangling or stabbing seems almost humane.

Besides Cordelia there is only one woman in all of James's work who evokes a really positive response: Aunt Jane Dalgleish. Nearly everyone else is fussy, neurotic, sadistic, simple, scheming, or evil. They are, on the whole, a depressing lot.

A SENSE OF STYLE

"Civilized," "literate," and "complex" are just a few of the adjectives that are frequently used to describe P.D. James's writing. Her style is all of that; it is very English, very intelligent, and above all very readable.

Central to the whole concept of the mystery is, of course, plot. Is it logical? Believable? Clear, or muddled? The success of the story depends to a great degree on the answers to these questions. Agatha Christie became the most popular mystery writer in history on the basis of her convoluted plots and surprise endings, although she was not a great writer in the usually accepted sense. That didn't matter. She excelled in the one area where excellence is demanded.

While P.D. James does not create the same kind of plots as Christie did, James too excels in this all-important category. All the other writing skills she possesses—and they are many—would not have saved her as a mystery writer if she didn't build tight plots.

The mystery format demands that there be a crime, several

suspects, numerous clues scattered here and there, and a detective capable of finding, analyzing, and interpreting them. If, along the way, the reader finds himself following some false trails, so much the better.

From her very first novel, James has succeeded in this difficult task. *Cover Her Face* is a typical mystery, its murder taking place early and the solving of it proceeding step by tiny step. The reader attempting to follow Dalgleish's thinking may find himself distracted by the third-person narrative style, for James is as often describing the thoughts of the suspects as she is her detective's. Carefully worded thought sequences can (and do) divert attention from the real culprit.

A Mind to Murder is even better done, as two separate crimes are made to seem related and thereby throw suspicion entirely upon the blackmailer—Nagle—and away from Marion Bolam, the murderer.

Shroud for a Nightingale, An Unsuitable Job for a Woman, and *Death of an Expert Witness* are equally well plotted, with clues abounding, but false leads constantly tempting the reader away from the main path. When the solutions are presented, they seem to be the logical results of the various characters' personalities; they are, therefore, essentially believable as opposed to just possible.

Unnatural Causes and *The Black Tower* are not so well constructed, and both suffer from melodramatic excess. Oddly enough, however, it is these two books that contain some of James's very best characterizations, especially those of ill or handicapped people, and the slightly imperfect plots are carried along on the strength of these character studies.

In all cases, even where a story is marred by melodrama, the plot is intricately devised and presented in an orderly manner. Clues are often subtle and derived as much from personality as from physical evidence. There are always enough "red herrings" to complicate things and make for genuine puzzlement.

Her methods of murder are many, and they range from the mundane—strangling, for example—to such ingenious horrors as disinfectant in the intragastric feed. Poison is a rare choice. When she does use it, it is not an unknown variety but something more common, such as nicotine. She is careful to set such use in a hospital or clinic setting, where the murderer has both knowledge of and access to poisonous substances. Even in this she strives for verisimilitude.

Motivation is important to James, and she has often said that her fictional crimes are the natural result of the situations she creates. While she does give people a variety of reasons for murder, she relies somewhat too heavily on one device: the will. In *A Mind to Murder*, in *Unnatural Causes*, in *An Unsuitable Job for a Woman*, in *The Black Tower* and even *Death of an Expert Witness*, the question of inheritance is crucial to the plot.

Pace is important to a novel, and James manages to keep her story moving, despite a paucity of action. Psychological movement is more crucial than physical. There are no fast fists, no cracking guns; rather, there is a careful unfolding of personality, a meticulous placing of detail.

James's skill at characterization has already been discussed. She is a master. Her major characters are many-layered, and she can make her minor ones memorable with only a sentence or two.

Equally impressive is her ability to create atmosphere and mood. Whether she is writing about a clinic in London or a nursing home in East Anglia, she paints a vivid and complete picture, filled with interesting detail and brilliantly alive with minutiae. Much of this can be traced to the fact that she writes about what she knows, the health and hospital field, and, more recently, police administration. From long years of experience on many levels in both of these areas, James has amassed a store of knowledge from which to draw, and her ability to set it down clearly makes her very strong indeed in this area.

But, besides knowing how a hospital works and understanding the various levels of administration as well as basic medical facts, James has a natural descriptive ability that extends to other areas as well. She can bring a street, a house, or an event to life with accurate and well-chosen words.

One of her passions, she has admitted, is Georgian architecture, and she manages to put a Georgian building into almost every one of her books. Her interest in architecture lends itself to competent description of other buildings, too. Whatever the style, she enjoys telling about it:

> The house itself was one of a Georgian terrace. It stood at the south corner of the square, comfortable, unpretentious and wholly pleasing.

At the rear a narrow passage ran into Lincoln Square Mews. There was a railed basement; in front of the house the railings curved on each side of the broad steps which led to the door and supported two wrought-iron lamp standards. On the right of the door an unpretentious bronze plaque bore the name . . . "The Steen Clinic."

The house was an excellent example of late 17th century domestic architecture, a three-story brick mansion with a hipped roof and four dormer windows, the center three-bay projection surmounted by a pediment with a richly carved cornice and medallions. A flight of four wide, curved stone steps led to the doorway, imposing on its pilasters but solidly, unostentatiously right. Dalgleish paused momentarily to study the facade . . .

In *Death of an Expert Witness* she describes a modern house, owned by Maxim Howarth and Domenica Schofield:

Howarth's house was three miles outside Chevisham village . . . a modern building of concrete, wood, and glass cantilevered above the flat fenlands, with two white wings like folded sails. Even in the fading light it was impressive. The house stood in uncompromising and splendid isolation, depending for its effect on nothing but perfection of line and artful simplicity. . . . As they made their way up the open-tread, carved wooden stairs Dalgleish complimented him on the house. Howarth said:

"It was designed by a Swedish architect . . ."

James is not without humor in her descriptions of homes. Like most people who appreciate good architecture, she has a horror of bad design. In *Cover Her Face* she writes of both the Proctors' and the Pullens' homes with a hint of shock:

Rose Cottage . . . was a late 18th-century labourer's cottage with enough superficial charm and antiquity to tempt the passing motorist to an opinion that something could be made of it. In the Pullens' hands something had, a replica of a thousand urban council houses. A large plaster model of an Alsatian dog occupied all the window space in the front room. Behind it the lace curtains were elegantly draped and tied with blue ribbon. . . . One wall was papered with a design of pink stars against a blue background. The opposite wall was painted in matching pink . . .

A row of identical houses stretched as far as the eye could see. Although they were identical in structure however, they were very different in appearance for hardly two of the small front gardens were alike. All were carefully sown and tended. A few householders had expressed their individuality with . . . coy stone gnomes fishing from basins. . . . The curtains showed signs of careful if misguided choosing . . . and were supplemented by additional half-curtains of draped lace or net which were carefully drawn against the curiosity of a vulgar world.

Not only buildings but entire villages spring to life under P.D. James's pen. The little writer's colony at Monksmere, in Suffolk, is painted stone by stone, each cottage carefully placed along the rough track that served as a road, heather fading and gorse in bloom, woodsmoke mingling with the salt smell of the sea, crisp and pungent in the October air. One can almost feel the dried grasses under one's feet and hear the cries of the gulls as they circle the headland.

James frequently visits such seaside places along England's coast and knows them well. She is not a naturalist, but it is obvious she loves the outdoors. Her descriptions of scenery and of individual plants and birds are authentic. Her flowers never bloom at the wrong season nor in the wrong habitat; her birds are correct to the last feather.

Nowhere is this more true than in the birding scenes in *Unnatural Causes*. Whether "discussing . . . whether the avocet was likely to nest that year" or describing a flock of shorebirds to her nephew, Aunt Jane Dalgleish knows her birds:

"But what do you make of these?"
A small flock of grey-brown waders was twittering on the edge of the shingle. Before Dalgleish had time to note more than their white rumps and blackish, down-turned beaks, the birds rose in one swift direct flight and faded into the wind like a wisp of thin white smoke.
"Dunlin?" he hazarded.
"I thought you might say dunlin. They're very similar. No, those were curlew-sandpipers."
"But the last time you showed me a curlew-sandpiper it had pink plumage," protested Dalgleish.
"That was last summer. In the autumn they take on the buffish plumage of the young birds . . ."

No one but an expert knows—or cares—about the summer and winter plumages of curlew-sandpipers, and how they compare to dunlin. Only a really experienced "birder" would make special note of the white rump patch that is the definitive difference between the two. But that is precisely the point. Aunt Jane *is* an expert—that has already been established. She most certainly would know and care which species she was seeing and would point it out to Adam. The conversation is totally in character and, most importantly, the information put forth in that paragraph is totally accurate.

James has a passing acquaintance with shorebirds like those she has described, but is not an expert herself, and she admitted that she checked the information with ornithologists before attributing it to Aunt Jane. "I always do that, whenever I am not personally certain of something," she said. "I strive for total accuracy."

She usually achieves it. In another book about another coast (*The Black Tower*, set in Dorset), she writes of Dennis Lerner, a male nurse whose avocation is geology. Dalgleish knows of his interest and asks him about a particular section of cliff:

> "It's fascinating, isn't it? I love the variety of this coast. You get the same shale further to the west at Kimmeridge; there it's known as Kimmeridge coal. It's bituminous you know, you can actually burn it . . . the blackstone looks a bit dull and uninteresting now, but if it's polished with beeswax it comes up like jet. . . . People used to make ornaments of it as far back as Roman times . . ."

Earlier in that book Dalgleish had walked alone on the headland, through "a tatter of bronzed bracken"

> crumpled with the wind, and low tangles of bramble bushes, their red and black berries tight and meagre compared with the luscious fruit of inland hedgerows. The headland was . . . studded with small limestone rocks . . .

During that walk, when Dalgleish notes "the brief metallic warble and churling note of stonechats, busy among the brambles; a solitary black-headed gull motionless as a ship's figurehead on a promontory . . . ," the reader can be certain that first of all, stonechats can be found in Dorset in early October, and second, that they make a "brief metallic warble."

Attention to such detail is perhaps a minor matter in a book that is primarily concerned with a tightly constructed murder mystery plot, but it is in truth very important from James's own point of view. She is not concerned simply with the construction of a puzzle that exists separately and apart from its setting. She wants her people and places to be, above all, credible, and to achieve that end she must describe them with a clarity and accuracy that can withstand scrutiny. To fail in one aspect of her job would be, ultimately, to diminish the power of all of it. But she doesn't fail; instead, she has built a solid reputation for descriptive accuracy, from the internal workings of a hospital to the field marks of a bird.

One thing that is always marked in a discussion of James's style is her "literacy." Critics hail her as being "in the great British tradition" of writers whose people, middle and upper class, discuss art and quote poetry, even as they concoct devilish ways to do each other in. The lower classes, with their uneducated accents and ungrammatical speech, have little place in her pages, and when she does include some as minor characters— such as Black Shirl and Marlene in *Innocent Blood*—they are not thoroughly believable. Their words, it is evident, do not come easily from her pen.

James has a thorough grounding in literature. Although she never attended a university, she received what she has termed an "excellent" education at a girls' secondary school in Cambridge, and she sprinkles quotes and literary allusions throughout her books. She doesn't usually explain them, expecting her readers to understand. Those who don't will not find the story spoiled, but those who do will certainly find it enhanced.

A favorite device is to give her characters some of her own literary tastes. Her own favorite author, for example, is Jane Austen, whose "peace, sanity and order" she finds restful. It is not surprising that Adam Dalgleish, who after all does share some of his creator's likes and dislikes, prefers Jane Austen too and keeps at least one of her books on his bedside table at all times. Dalgleish and James share also a respect for Thomas Hardy and for the poet George Crabbe, whose work was being illustrated by Domenica Schofield in *Death of and Expert Witness*:

> Dalgleish said, "I've respected Crabbe ever since I read as a boy that Jane Austen said she could have fancied being Mrs. Crabbe. When he went to London for the first time he was so poor that he had to pawn all his clothes, and then he spent the money on an edition of Dryden's poems."

It helps to know that Crabbe is a transitional poet who linked eighteenth-century neoclassicism with nineteenth-century romanticism, though it really has nothing important to do with the plot of the story. It does, however, add one more layer to Dalgleish— and to Domenica.

In the same book Brenda Pridmore shows that she, too, knows her Austen: "It was you who found me, wasn't it? I remember being picked up—rather like Marianne Dashwood in *Sense and Sensibility*—and the nice tweedy smell of your jacket."

Jane Austen and Thomas Hardy are also Cordelia Gray's favorites (She doesn't mention Crabbe), and Cordelia can also quote Blake at will.

> "He left a note but not an explanation . . .
> "Down the winding cavern we groped our tedious way, till a void boundless as the nether sky appeared . . ."
> "You claim to be a detective, Miss Gray. What do you deduce from that?"
> "That your son read William Blake. Isn't it a passage from *The Marriage of Heaven and Hell?*"

James likes to describe characters by describing the contents of their bookshelves. Jo Fallon, the student nurse who was murdered in *Shroud for a Nightingale*, had

> A collection of modern poetry, his own last volume included; a complete set of Jane Austen . . . about two dozen paperbacks of modern popular novels, Greene, Waugh, Compton Burnett, Hartley, Powell, Cary. But most of the books were poetry. Looking at them, he thought, we shared the same tastes. If we had met we should at least have had something to say to each other. "Everyman's death diminishes me." But of course, Doctor Donne.

Mark Callendar had "several volumes of the *Cambridge Modern History*; some Trollope and Hardy; a complete William Blake . . ." Like most of the others, Mark's books reflect James's own personal preferences.

Hardy is mentioned yet another time, as James describes the London offices of Father Baddeley's solicitors in *The Black Tower*: "It was a house in which any of Hardy's more prosperous characters would have felt themselves at home . . ."

James's literary interests are not confined to the past. She can

drop modern names as easily as older ones, as when she has
Frederica Saxon say of Enid Bolam, "Who would suppose that
Bolam would want to see Anouilh? I suppose she was sent a free
ticket."

Cordelia Gray gains some information through her knowledge
of modern theater. Hugo, Sophia, Davie, and Isabelle have told
her that, on the night Mark died, they were all at the Arts Theater
watching Pinter. She acts on a hunch and says to Isabelle:

> "Did you enjoy the Pinter? Weren't you frightened by that dreadful
> last scene when Wyatt Gillman is gunned down by the natives?"
> It was so easy that Cordelia almost despised herself . . .
> "Oh no, I did not care about it, I was not frightened. I was with
> Hugo and the others, you see."
> Cordelia turned to Hugo Tilling.
> "Your friend doesn't seem to know the difference between Pinter
> and Osborne."

Isabelle may not, but P.D. James certainly does, and she expects
that her readers will too.

Nor does James slight earlier writers, those of the seventeenth
century. Her very first title, *Cover Her Face*, comes from Webster's
Duchess of Malfi (c. 1613), and she refers again to the Jacobean
period in *Death of an Expert Witness*, as Maxim Howarth reflects on
his love for his sister Domenica, a love of which his own wife was
jealous and of which Dom's husband was painfully aware:

> He remembered Charles Schofield's gauze-cocooned head, the dying
> eyes still malicious behind two slits in the bandages, the swollen lips
> painfully moving.
> "Congratulations, Giovanni. Remember me in your garden in
> Parma."
> What had been so astounding was . . . that he had hated his brother-
> in-law enough to die with that taunt on his lips. Or had he taken it
> for granted that a physicist, poor philistine, wouldn't know his
> Jacobean dramatists?

The play thus obliquely referred to is John Ford's *'Tis Pity She's
a Whore* (c. 1627), a tragedy about the fatal attraction of Giovanni
for his sister Annabella. The play takes place, of course, in Parma.
None of this is explained, however, by James, who assumes that
the reader will be as well-read and as thoroughly educated as she
is herself.

At times it appears James is simply having fun. Julia Pardoe, for instance, is a relatively minor character in *Shroud for a Nightingale*, one of the student nurses, but the really astute reader may know that Julia Pardoe was also a nineteenth-century English author of travel books and essays on French history. It doesn't matter, but it is interesting.

Some may find this intellectual game-playing an annoyance. A degree in English should not be a prerequisite for enjoying a murder mystery. But to the initiated such allusions add greatly to the color of the piece. To James's credit, it must be stated that these literary asides are never intrusive, nor are they ever crucial to the plot.

The same can be said of her occasional untranslated foreign phrases, often in Latin. It may once have been true that every educated person could understand at least the rudiments of that language, but it is no longer. It is, however, for James's characters: "'You'll last for me until the day I die. *Contra mundum*'. It was too late now to sever that cord even if he wanted to."

Probably everyone will understand what Mary Taylor means when she explains to Dalgleish that she must act *in loco parentis*, but many will miss Sister Rolfe's meaning when she says, ". . . *Nil nisi* and all that, but the girl was just a prig . . ."

Nil nisi comes from *De mortuis nil nisi bonum*: "Speak nothing but good of the dead." Similarly, in *The Black Tower*, she doesn't translate when Dalgleish comes upon the gravestone of the first Wilfred Anstey and reads: "CONCEPTIO CULPA NASCI PENA LABOR VITA NECESSI MORI." His thoughts on these heady phrases clarify them only slightly for the reader who doesn't know Latin.

Equally often she throws in some French. In *Death of an Expert Witness*, there is a memorial in the Wren Chapel, which reads, "*Dieu aye merci de son ame*," and James does not add that this means, "May God have mercy on his soul." In the same book Maxim Howarth tells Dalgleish that his sister suffers from "*horreur de domicile*," while in *Shroud for a Nightingale* the description of Mary Taylor's room includes "a group of *objets trouvés*." None of these phrases is important; like the literary references, they add color to the story and permit the reader who does comprehend them to feel a sense of erudite comradeship with the author.

For nearly everyone, however, James's writing is a pleasure to read: colorful, clear, precise, ample without being padded, often dryly humorous, insightful, compassionate, kind. That she understands her characters, there is never any doubt. It is obvious, too, that she has a psychologist's comprehension of human nature, with an ability to put herself in the other person's mind, to feel his emotions and predict his actions. Such is her power of description that the reader will often sympathize with a "bad" character because he has been made aware of the complex motivations that lie behind every action. She does not sketch in black and white; indeed, her character studies might be titled, "Variations on a Shade of Gray." There's good—and bad—in everyone.

Sally Jupp, secretive and conniving, was a caring mother to her little son while her murderer, Mrs. Maxie, was the very essence of the country gentlewoman until she committed the ultimate crime. Enid Bolam loved her girl guides; Marion Bolam loved her mother. Brumfett was devoted to Mary Taylor; Mary Taylor was devoted to the care of her patients. In book after book James paints her characters in depth, and they emerge—like most real people— neither wholly good nor wholly bad.

When all James's books have been read, their plots analyzed and criticized, their characters studied, their solutions revealed, there are a few phrases that will invariably linger in the mind. Some are poignant: the words of Sylvia Kedge and Nell Kerrison, for example. But others are witty. Jane Austen herself would have been pleased to write, of Jane Dalgleish's mother, "She disliked the sight of other people's grief since it rendered them temporarily more interesting than herself."

James's sense of humor is obvious when she says of the John Carpendar Hospital, "The principles governing the menu planning were invariable. Liver and kidneys were never served on the days when the urinary surgeon operated . . ."

Perhaps most indicative of James's own mood is the generally upbeat way in which she ends her stories. Hers are not the kind of mysteries that build up to an O. Henry twist on the final page and leave the reader breathless. On the contrary, the action moves to a climax, the mystery is solved, and then the story winds down gently, with all loose ends tied. There is an almost nineteenth-century nicety about the way she puts everything in place at the end. And in almost all cases the bad are punished, and the good, if not rewarded, at least left to continue their lives in peace.

It has already been stated that James's strong feelings about criminal behavior require her to punish wrongdoers, by an "act of God" if not by the law. This satisfies her need for retribution, although it may seem too "fictional" for a story that purports to depict real life. In a like manner she has, in most of her books, added essentially unnecessary information about marriages, job changes, and various positive moves for many of her main characters. In *Cover Her Face* Dalgleish meets Deborah several months after the murder and discovers that Catherine Bowers is going to marry James Ritchie, that Felix Hearne has emigrated to Canada, and that Stephen Maxie (a doctor) "is at hospital most of the time, and terribly busy." *A Mind to Murder* has Mrs. Shorthouse, the clinic's cleaning woman, calling Dalgleish to report that Miss Saxon "is going to work in a home for subnormal kids up north," while Miss Priddy has been transferred, and Mrs. Bolam is in a nursing home.

As recently as *The Black Tower*, her sixth book, there is a very positive ending, with a strong hint of a future relationship between Dalgleish and Cordelia. Only *Death of an Expert Witness* fails to reflect James's generally optimistic outlook on life. Since the publication of that book James has stepped beyond the narrow confines of the mystery form to write *Innocent Blood*, a novel that deals with crime but is not in itself a mystery. She is now squarely in the mainstream of popular fiction. Her great commercial success in that area, however, will not put an end to her mystery career. She admits to being "extremely fond" of the mystery form. She finds working within the genre's strict rules very challenging and will, she has stated, "certainly be doing it again."

NOTES

References are identified by the page number and a few key words of each quotation.

CHAPTER 1

PAGE	QUOTE	SOURCE
2	I feared	P.D. James, interview, *New York Times*, December 11, 1977.
2	It is the essential	Ibid.
3	a "real" detective	"PW Interviews: P.D. James," *Publishers' Weekly*, January 5, 1976.
5	favorite author	P.D. James, interview, *New York Times*, December 11, 1977.

CHAPTER 5

75	Of course I disapproved	*Cover Her Face*, p. 93.
75	Isn't that a Stubbs?	Ibid., p. 100.

141

PAGE	QUOTE	SOURCE
76	She didn't know what she expected	*A Mind to Murder*, p. 62.
76	he wasn't trying to irritate	*Ibid.*, p. 76.
77	the extraordinary one	*Death of An Expert Witness*, p. 178.
78	it came to him	*Unnatural Causes*, p. 10.
79	Who teaches you?	*A Mind to Murder*, p. 159.
79	there was only one picture	*Shroud for a Nightingale*, p. 49.
79	the oil over the mantelpiece	*Death of An Expert Witness*, p. 198.
80	The pianist	*A Mind to Murder*, p. 165.
80	bedside Jane Austen	*Unnatural Causes*, p. 213.
81	[the facts] were seldom discovered	*The Black Tower*, p. 58.
82	prying among	*A Mind to Murder*, p. 149.
82	He was too reticent	*Shroud for a Nightingale*, p. 204.
82	His job, in which	*A Mind to Murder*, p. 225.
82	What would a man	*Shroud for a Nightingale*, p. 282.

CHAPTER 6

94	He wished he could feel sorry	*Unnatural Causes*, p. 93.
94	We all suffer from a progressive	*The Black Tower*, p. 51.
94	Mrs. Meakin, what you are doing	*Death of an Expert Witness*, p. 286.
95	[Grace Willison] thought about	*The Black Tower*, p. 184.
95	Death, thought Dalgleish	*Death of an Expert Witness*, p. 176.
96	Thinking of her father and Bernie	*An Unsuitable Job for a Woman*, p. 191.
96	I ought to dislike her less	*Cover Her Face*, p. 69.
96	if people died	*Ibid.*, p. 147.
97	Necessi mori	*The Black Tower*, p. 108.
97	The police are	P.D. James, interview with Jack O'Brien, WOR, May 21, 1980.
98	He had never yet apologized	*Cover Her Face*, p. 254.
98	I wonder just how good	*A Mind to Murder*, p. 254.
99	If they concern themselves	P.D. James, WOR interview, May 21, 1980.
101	dreadful, unspeakable	P.D. James, telephone interview with author, June 6, 1980.

CHAPTER 7

PAGE	QUOTE	SOURCE
105	Likeable people	P.D. James, telephone interview with author, June 6, 1980.
106	Get to know the dead person	*An Unsuitable Job for a Woman*, p. 43.
106	She enjoyed the feeling	*Cover Her Face*, p. 237.
114	I can make relationships	*Death of an Expert Witness*, p. 221.
115	like an animal	Ibid., p. 339.
116	many generations	Ibid., p. 101.
116	My God, yours is a filthy trade	Ibid., p. 339.
116	drab, sallow-faced	Ibid., p. 282.
116	bringing into the room	Ibid., p. 174.
117	had a curious habit	Ibid., p. 302.
120	the happiest marriages	*Shroud for a Nightingale*, p. 6.
120	[at the theater]	*Unnatural Causes*, p. 99.
121	They're a spiteful lot	Ibid., p. 51.
123	he liked her	*A Mind to Murder*, p. 191.
123	This ambition	Ibid., p. 36.
123	carefully spaced encounters	*The Black Tower*, p. 8.
126	Being a man	*A Mind to Murder*, p. 145.
126	You should have had	*Unnatural Causes*, p. 36.
126	What is there	*An Unsuitable Job for a Woman*, p. 238.

CHAPTER 8

131	The house itself	*A Mind to Murder*, p. 25.
132	The house was an excellent	*Death of an Expert Witness*, p. 106.
134	I always do that	P.D. James, telephone interview with the author, June 6, 1980.
135	peace, sanity and order	P.D. James, interview, *New York Times*, December 11, 1977.
136	He left a note	*An Unsuitable Job for a Woman*, p. 74.
137	Who would suppose	*A Mind to Murder*, p. 187.
137	Did you enjoy the Pinter	*An Unsuitable Job for a Woman*, p. 106.
138	You'll last for me	*Death of an Expert Witness*, p. 222.

PAGE	QUOTE	SOURCE
138	*Nil nisi* and all that	*Shroud for a Nightingale*, p. 134.
138	*horreur de domicile*	*Death of an Expert Witness*, p. 206.
139	She disliked the sight	*Unnatural Causes*, p. 12.
139	The principles governing	*Shroud for a Nightingale*, p. 128.
140	extremely fond	P.D. James, telephone interview with author, June 6, 1980.
140	certainly be doing it again	Ibid.

BIBLIOGRAPHY

I. NOVELS BY P.D. JAMES

Cover Her Face. New York: Scribner, 1966.
A Mind to Murder. New York: Scribner, 1967.
Unnatural Causes. New York: Scribner, 1967.
Shroud for a Nightingale. New York: Scribner, 1971.
An Unsuitable Job for a Woman. New York: Scribner, 1973.
The Black Tower. New York Scribner, 1975.
Death of an Expert Witness. New York: Scribner, 1977.
Crime Times Three (*Cover Her Face, A Mind to Murder, Shroud for a Nightingale*). New York: Scribner, 1979.
Innocent Blood. New York: Scribner, 1980.

II. NONFICTION BY P.D. JAMES WITH THOMAS A. CRITCHLEY

The Maul and the Pear Tree. London: Constable, 1971.

145

III. GENERAL ARTICLES ABOUT P.D. JAMES AND HER CHARACTERS

Bannon, Barbara, ed. "PW Interviews: P.D. James," *Publishers Weekly*, v. 209, January 5, 1976, pp. 8–9.

Cannon, M. "Mistress of Malice Domestic," *Macleans*, v. 93, June 30, 1980, p. 50.

Goddard, Donald. "The Unmysterious P.D. James," *The New York Times Book Review*, v. 85, April 27, 1980, p. 28.

James, P.D. "Ought Adam to Marry Cordelia," in Dilys Wynn, ed., *Murder Ink*. New York: Workman, 1977, p. 68.

Lask, Thomas. "Another Aspect of a Mystery Writer," *The New York Times*, February 8, 1980, p. 27.

The New York Times, Interview. December 11, 1977, p. 86.

de la Torre, Lillian. "Cordelia Gray: The Thinking Man's Heroine," in Dilys Wynn, ed., *Murderess Ink*. New York: Workman, 1977, pp. 113–116.

Winks, R.W. "Murder and Dying," *New Republic*, v. 175, July 31, 1976, pp. 31–32.

IV. SELECTED REVIEWS OF P.D. JAMES'S BOOKS

A. *COVER HER FACE*
   Best Sellers, v. 26, July 15, 1966.
   Books Today, v. 3, September 4, 1966.
   Kliatt Paperback Book Guide, v. 11, Winter 1977.
   Library Journal, v. 91, August 1966.
   The New York Times Book Review, v. 71, July 24, 1966.

B. *A MIND TO MURDER*
   Best Sellers, v. 26, March 1, 1967.
   Books Today, v. 4, April 2, 1967.
   Library Journal, v. 92, April 1, 1967.
   The New York Times Book Review, March 12, 1967.
   New Yorker, v. 43, March 11, 1967.
   Publishers Weekly, v. 191, February 6, 1967.
   Publishers Weekly, v. 210, September 13, 1976.
   Spectator, v. 236, June 12, 1976.
   Times Literary Supplement, December 13, 1974.

C. *UNNATURAL CAUSES*
   Best Sellers, v. 27, January 15, 1968.
   Kirkus, v. 35, September 1, 1967.

Manchester Guardian, v. 96, June 1, 1967.
Publishers Weekly, v. 192, August 14, 1967.
Punch, v. 252, May 10, 1967.
Spectator, v. 236, June 12, 1976.
Times Literary Supplement, May 18, 1967.

D. *SHROUD FOR A NIGHTINGALE*
   Best Sellers, v. 31, November 15, 1971.
   Booklist, v. 68, January 1, 1972.
   Critic, v. 30, March 1972.
   Library Journal, v. 97, January 1, 1972.
   The New York Times Book Review, January 16, 1972.
   The New York Times Book Review, June 4, 1972.
   Observer, June 13, 1971.
   Times Literary Supplement, October 22, 1971.

E. *AN UNSUITABLE JOB FOR A WOMAN*
   Best Sellers, v. 33, April 15, 1973.
   Book World (Washington Post), April 15, 1973.
   Critic, v. 32, September–October 1973.
   Kirkus, v. 41. January 15, 1973.
   Library Journal, v. 98, April 1, 1973.
   Ms., v. 2, April 1974.
   The New York Times Book Review, April 22, 1973.
   The New York Times Book Review, December 2, 1973.
   New Yorker, v. 49, July 23, 1973.
   Observer, November 5, 1972.
   Publishers Weekly, v. 203, January 29, 1973.
   Publishers Weekly, v. 208, August 18, 1975.
   Saturday Review: Art, April 1973.
   Spectator, v. 229, December 23, 1972.
   Times Literary Supplement, December 8, 1972.
   Wilson Library Bulletin, v. 47, June 1973.

F. *THE BLACK TOWER*
   Best Sellers, v. 35, September 1975.
   Booklist, v. 72, September 15, 1975.
   Books and Bookmen, v. 20, July 1975.
   Kirkus, v. 43, May 15, 1975.
   Library Journal, v. 100, July 1975.
   Listener, v. 93, June 5, 1975.
   The New York Times Book Review, November 23, 1975.

Observer, May 4, 1975.
Publishers Weekly, v. 208, August 18, 1975.
Publishers Weekly, v. 210, July 5, 1976.
Times Literary Supplement, July 11, 1975.
Village Voice, v. 20, December 15, 1975.

G. *DEATH OF AN EXPERT WITNESS*
Book World (Washington Post), November 20, 1977.
Book World (Washington Post), December 4, 1977.
Booklist, v. 74, December 15, 1977.
Contemporary Review, v. 235, July 1979.
Horn Book, v. 54, June 1978.
Kirkus, v. 45, September 1, 1977.
Library Journal, v. 102, November 1, 1977.
Listener, v. 99, March 23, 1978.
New Republic, v. 177, November 26, 1977.
The New York Times, November 15, 1977.
The New York Times Book Review, November 13, 1977.
New Yorker, March 6, 1978.
Newsweek, v, 91, January 23, 1978.
Observer, November 6, 1977.
Publishers Weekly, v. 212, September 19, 1977.
Publishers Weekly, v. 214, September 11, 1978.
Spectator, v. 239, December 3, 1977.
Time, v. 111, April 17, 1978.
Time Literary Supplement, November 4, 1977.
Village Voice, v. 23, December 18, 1978.

H. *CRIME TIMES THREE*
Booklist, v. 75, June 15, 1979.
Books of the Times, v. 2, July 1979.
Ms., v. 8, August 1979.
Wilson Library Bulletin, v. 53, April 1979.

I. *INNOCENT BLOOD*
America, v. 143, August 9, 1980.
Christian Science Monitor, June 25, 1980.
Library Journal, v. 105, April 15, 1980.
New Statesman, v. 99, May 9, 1980.
New York, v. 13, April 21, 1980.
New York Review of Books, v. 27, July 17, 1980.

The New York Times, May 7, 1980.
The New York Times Book Review, April 27, 1980.
New Yorker, v. 56, June 23, 1980.
Newsweek, v. 95, May 12, 1980.
Time, v. 115, May 26, 1980.
Times Literary Supplement, March 21, 1980.

INDEX